# How to Think

Spencer K. Wright

Copyright © 2018 Spencer K. Wright
All rights reserved.
ISBN: 1986747069
ISBN-13: 978-1986747066


Cover Photo: *Daydream*
Copyright © 2018 Spencer K. Wright
All rights reserved.

For Sophie, who is brilliant beyond her years.
May the world learn from your mirth and wit.

Acknowledgements

A heartfelt thank you to my editors, Drewie Knuwie, et al., who each sacrificed in their own way in order to assist me. Without their tireless efforts, this work would not be possible. Also, a special thank you to George, Scott, Brady, and Lee, who have each taught me something important about the nature of thinking. Finally, a warm thank you to the many individuals who have provided opposing viewpoints to me throughout my life. There is simply no way I could have learned to think without you.

# Introduction

### About this book

The United States minted a penny in 1792, one of the first coins of the new nation, with a picture of Lady Liberty. Contrary to what might be supposed by many today, the phrase "In God We Trust" was not printed anywhere on it. (The earliest that phrase was used was 1864.) Instead, curving around the rim of the penny were the words, "Liberty Parent of Science and Industry." Neglecting to mention God on the currency wasn't some secret act of rebellion against the religious inclinations of the American public. It was actually Founding Fathers, Thomas Jefferson and George Washington, who discussed the design through letters before it was presented to Congress for a vote.

What "We the People" chose to honor on their first currency should tell us something about the priorities of that first generation of Americans. They weren't looking to enshrine God; they were looking to enshrine what they believed were the true founding principles of the country. The founders of the US were actually rebels who had just declared independence against an authoritarian government only a decade or so earlier. Part of that revolt was driven by the desire to be free of the crown; the other was to be free of religious persecution. Thomas Jefferson saw both political and religious power as abusive over the mind of man. From his perspective, the founding of the United States was never about setting up a Christian nation, but was about creating a land where all were free to think and believe as they wished. He saw compulsory faith-based thinking as antithetical to freedom. He also saw many faith-based thoughts themselves as antithetical to reason.

> "History, I believe, furnishes no example of a priest-ridden people maintaining a free civil government." ~ Thomas Jefferson, Letter to Alexander von Humboldt, 6 December 1813
>
> "Ridicule is the only weapon which can be used against unintelligible propositions. Ideas must be distinct before reason can act upon them; and no man ever had a distinct idea of the trinity." ~ Thomas Jefferson, Letter to Francis Adrian Van der Kemp, 30 July 1816

Jefferson's animosity toward religion and inherited titles was, in large part, driven by the principles of the European Enlightenment, also frequently referred to as the "Age of Reason." The Enlightenment had swept through Europe during the 1700s with thinkers who took the bold step of confronting the despotic powers of the Roman Catholic church as well as the ruling monarchies of the time. But the notion of governments "by the People" were untrusted generally. There were even a number of debates leading up to the founding of democracies such as the United States and France, arguing that only a "natural aristocracy" of inherited titles can maintain power. In other words, the status quo believed "the People" were not fit to govern themselves. The Enlightenment upended these traditions with principles such as constitutional democracies, individual liberty, and religious freedom.

While the Enlightenment philosophy formed the foundation of American ideals, within a few decades, a contrary movement formed to push back against the Enlightenment known as Romanticism. Enlightenment thinking emphasized rational thinking and science. Romanticism emphasized emotion and intuition over reason. Romanticism also grew out of fears that the new industrial revolution and explaining the mystery of nature were taking all the fun out of life. Romanticism decided it didn't really like concrete answers to questions about life. It preferred mystery. And so it positioned itself as an ANTI-INTELLECTUAL response to the intellectualism of Enlightenment thinking.

And these two competing philosophies have been battling

one another ever since. There is an unavoidable tension of sorts because these modes of thinking require adherence to contradictory principles. Enlightenment looks for an empirical explanation; Romanticism eschews explanation in favor of mystery. Enlightenment seeks to understand how a thing is; Romanticism seeks to understand how one wishes it to be. Are there fairies at the bottom of the garden? Enlightenment thinking says to look and answer the question based on observation. Romanticism says there are fairies if you believe hard enough.

These two modes of thought have been in a "cold war" of sorts ever since. They maintain an uneasy ceasefire, but always maneuvering and plotting against one another for dominance in the public's mind. There have been many attempts to reconcile the two, to demonstrate a compatibility between these distinct ways of thinking. And while commonalities exist, there are simply too many ways in which they are diametrically opposed. In any case, the pendulum's swing between these two general ways of thinking has gone back and forth multiple times since then, and it was all fine and well...until Enlightenment thinking decided to build a nuke.

In retrospect, it wasn't very nice of Enlightenment thinking to do that. Romanticism would have never done such a thing, but in fairness, it couldn't have built nukes even if it had tried. You can't build a nuke by wishing reality worked a certain way. You actually have to understand the physical properties of matter at the atomic scale. It takes Enlightenment thinking to create such a thing. Either way, here we are...with nukes.

Of course, nukes are a metaphor for the multiplicity of ways humanity can bring about its own demise. They're not the only way we can kill ourselves. The modern world, brought about by Enlightenment thinking, now has many tools of destruction at our disposal. Since the beginning of recorded history, the fastest way to travel was by horse. Since the time of the Enlightenment, humanity has broken the sound barrier and travelled to the moon and back. The world is completely different than it was 200 years ago. The tools we have are bigger and inherently more dangerous. Tools aren't inherently good or bad. But they need to be understood. Rationally.

But instead, the threat of globalization has caused a resurgence of Romanticism, and the specter of anti-intellectualism has reached the highest political offices of government. The world is scary and hard to understand. But the solution to the problem is not to pretend that reality works differently than it does. The solution is NOT to remove science from public policy and public funding.

The solution is to understand how reality actually works, and work according to the actual rules of nature. Anti-intellectualism might have been tolerable as a political force in the 1800s, but our tools of destruction are too powerful today. We are not going to survive with a collective philosophy of appeal to emotion, intuition and hoping reality works the way we wish it would. And that's why we need the tools of this book.

Recently, there has been an increased push to treat Romanticism as compatible and in alignment with Enlightenment thinking, all the while enacting anti-intellectual policies in the government. The time has come to take a step back and see how these philosophies are not simply different but contradictory. We need to commit to understand reality as it really is and to follow reason even if it contradicts our Romantic beliefs about reality. The purpose of this book is to disentangle these two philosophies so we can see each clearly for what it is. Rational-based thinking is not the same as faith-based thinking. Without a doubt, they are *different* ways of thinking. But more importantly, they are *contradictory* in many ways. We need to stop pretending that there is a harmony between them when there isn't. We need to ensure that we, the People, know HOW TO THINK, and then enact sound policy based on reason.

## A useful list of logical fallacies

Throughout this book, I'll be discussing many logical fallacies. Logical fallacies are errors in reasoning, and if your goal is to be reasonable, you should avoid using them. One of the first steps to proper thinking is to learn how to avoid using logical fallacies. This is an important part of thinking. But as I was writing the book, I realized that breaking to explain each logical fallacy totally messed with my Zen flow. So instead, I decided to *cough* the logical fallacy under my breath and continue. If you are new to the fallacy and need a reference, I've listed most of them here with a useful example of how the fallacy works. But all of these are readily available on the Internet. Feel free to look up the various fallacies and commit to avoid using them in your reasoning.

### Appeal to Authority fallacy

Just because an authority figure says something, that doesn't make it true. Just because a trained, educated person with lots of credentials says something, that doesn't make it true. Educated people should have, with all of their training, better access to the facts. Appeal to the facts as much as possible, not the person.

### Appeal to Tradition fallacy

This fallacy is similar to Appeal to Authority. Just because Thomas Jefferson said something, that doesn't mean it's true. Do you see how we have a fallacy of sorts in the earlier section by appealing to Thomas Jefferson? Did you catch that at the time? My point there was actually a sort of anti-Appeal to Tradition. Many people believe Thomas Jefferson thought a certain way...it's useful to learn he didn't think like that to help disrupt that Appeal to Tradition.

### Argument from Ignorance

This fallacy doesn't mean someone is ignorant/stupid. It means that if you don't know the facts about something then the void of knowledge is not an open invitation to start filling in the gaps with speculation. If you don't know then you don't know.

### Bandwagon fallacy

Everyone commits this fallacy. But so what? Even if everyone commits the fallacy, that doesn't make it okay to commit. Popular opinion doesn't make something right or wrong.

### Begging the Question / Circular Reasoning fallacy

The Bible is true because it was written by God. And how do I know it was written by God? Because it says so right there in the Bible, silly! If you conclude something, you need to appeal to something other than the conclusion to make your point. Otherwise, you've committed the Circular Reasoning fallacy

**Burden Shifting fallacy**

This is the best fallacy to commit. Don't believe me? Well, you can't prove this isn't the best fallacy to commit! If I make a claim, then the burden falls on me to support it, not you.

**Equivocation fallacy**

Roses are red, violets are blue (the color). I'm feeling blue (down in the dumps), therefore I'm a flower. Do you see how the word "blue" is being used in two very different ways? Using the same word to mean two different things, but treating it as though it's the same thing is equivocating the meaning of the word.

**No True Scotsman fallacy**

Person 1: No Scotsman puts sugar on their porridge.
Person 2: Well Hamish McGuiness does.
Person 1: Well, no TRUE Scotsman puts sugar on their porridge!
Changing the claim to exclude exceptions to your rule is committing this fallacy. Own your words. Admit when you're wrong.

### Non Sequitur fallacy

Roses are red, therefore Hamish McGuiness puts sugar on his porridge. Also, the truth of the second statement is in no way supported by the first statement. This is a non sequitur.

### Slippery Slope fallacy

Just because Romantics control the levers of power, that doesn't automatically mean they will destroy the world. It's a fallacy to say one bad thing will lead to the worst case scenario. Each slip of the slope needs to be supported by its own logic.

### Straw Man fallacy

Person 1: Cats should have lasers attached to their heads
Person 2: My opponent believes that cats should kill all of humanity and take over the world.
Person 1: That's not even close to what I just said.
When you are debating with others, make sure you can correctly restate their argument.

### Tu Quoque / Whatabouitsm fallacy

Person 1: You just stole an apple.
Person 2: Well, what about Tommy? He steals things all the time!
Granted, Tommy shouldn't steal either. This isn't about Tommy though. Don't try to get out of your fallacy by

turning the tables onto someone else.

### Texas Sharpshooter fallacy

If you're going to be rational, you gotta count your hits *and* misses. Intellectual integrity requires that you admit when you're wrong. Don't make claims and then draw targets around where your bullets landed.

# How to Think

Spencer K. Wright

# Chapter 1 – In the Beginning

All great books begin with a self-effacing joke about the miniscule reach of the audience. So if you're reading this you're either my editor, my publisher, or my mom. And since she's both my editor and publisher, my guess is she's trying to figure out how to avoid reading it too. (I love you, mom! But no, seriously, can you read it please?)

And now that we have that out of the way, let me introduce you to the greatest book ever conceived by a human mind. And even better, since it's only *human* minds I'm competing with, I obviously don't have to go up against any books written by God. So naturally I don't have to take on the Bible, the Quran, or the Book of Mormon! Whew! Okay, so here we begin our journey of the next best book ever written. What you are about to read is probably the fourth greatest book in the history of the world! How does that sound? You ready for this? Yeah, fourth is not a medal contender, but still respectable.

Anyway, unlike the big three, this book is going to teach you HOW TO THINK. You might be saying to yourself, "I already know how to think." And if you're reading this book, you're probably right. My guess is most people reading this book will be those who are already critical thinkers.  Let's face it, the audience of this book will probably be 99% preaching to the choir.  Most people want to read something that agrees with their preconceived biases (*cough* confirmation bias *cough*), and you're not different.  Don't feel bad...you're still special just like everyone else.  But we're probably all in the same boat on this one.  You probably picked up this book because you're pretty sure this book is going to support what you already believe.  Otherwise, you're likely steering clear of it.  But since you're reading this, that means you're already a thinker just like me!  Let's give each other a big hug, do the dance of joy, and tell one another how smart we are!  Because all great books start by flattering the audience.

Even though we already know how to think, there's still a YUGE market for this book, but unfortunately, chances are pretty slim someone who really needs this book is going to actually read it.  Fortunately for you, gentle reader, you already have the skills necessary to do exactly what this book is going to teach.  But maybe it'll give you some ideas for surreptitiously slipping some thinking skills into the conversation at Thanksgiving dinner or something like that.  Or it'll make a great stocking stuffer like The Clapper or a Chia Pet.

While I still think most people who read this book will be of above average intelligence, we need to pause from our self-congratulations to point out that actually *everyone* needs this book. Yes, you're smart and rational. But I've also never met anyone who utterly lacks any powers of rationality. In other words, everyone is rational to some degree, but everyone has room for improvement. When the pavement hits the fan, there's a lot of broken plastic everywhere. Oh wait, that's not how the metaphor goes. Anyway, where the rubber meets the road (i.e., when we interface with reality) most people understand the causal relationship between a light switch and a light. Yes, that takes a rational mind. (No, seriously it does.) And we've all got that. Nothing to be throwing a party over. We all get that certain actions cause certain results. We can think logically about it. And we can make rational decisions based on that. We know that falling out of the 12th story window of a building is going to seriously injure or kill us. We understand how to think about these things logically, in exactly the same way Einstein would think about it (*cough* appeal to authority fallacy *cough*). Almost every single person on the planet gets this.

But just because we're rational in one area of our lives, that doesn't mean we're consistent. Life makes us all into hypocrites. Where rationality breaks down for nearly all of us is the point where we have to defend our own biases. We already think we have a pretty good handle on smarts, so that means we're automatically smart in every other domain, amirite? (*cough* equivocation fallacy *cough*) If I understand the cause-and-effect relationship of a lightbulb, then of course I also understand the causal effect of climate science, too? Nope. One domain does not automatically or necessarily spill over into the other.

And nothing is truer in this regard than the highly intelligent religious person.

There is no bigger bias in the world than one's religious preference. Except perhaps one's political bias, or thinking that your grandkids are the cutest in the world. That last one isn't a bias...your grandkids really are, objectively, the cutest; don't let anyone tell you differently. (*cough* genetic fallacy, maybe? *cough* eh, maybe we'll come back to this). I've spent over twenty years investigating religious bias, with the most important investigation being my own. But before that, I spent years questioning the religious bias in others. It was *so easy* to see the bias when I was looking outward. But it was almost impossible to hold up a mirror to my own thinking. I'm a relatively intelligent guy, who also happened to be religious until a decade ago. But it's not like I wasn't smart before 10 years ago and then became smart, and then left my religion as a result of my newfound intelligence. Then why was it sooo hard to see my own biases, being a smart guy and all?

Well, first we need to get over the incorrect thinking that you can't be smart and religious. Of course you can be smart and religious. Many smart religious people even devote considerable effort to demonstrating that there are lots of other intelligent people who are also religious. You can have a PhD and believe in a god. I know this because I know many people who fit into both categories. I know doctors and lawyers and (okay, maybe lawyers are easier to explain...whoa! Take it easy...it's just a lawyer joke), and college professors who are all incredibly smart people who are also religious.

So yes, you can be smart and religious. But what I hope to convince you of in this book is that you can't think rational thoughts and faith-based thoughts at *precisely the same time*. You can only think one thing at a time. And so at any given moment you might be thinking a rational thought. Or you might be thinking a faith-based thought. But at that exact moment, you are never thinking both. And why is this? It's because faith-based thought and rational-based thought aren't simply *different* ways of thinking. They are *contradictory* ways of thinking.

Now, I know a lot of my highly intelligent religious friends are going to disagree with me on that last point. But just to make it clear, those last few sentences are the primary thesis of this entire book, so back off, give me some space and a couple of pages of text to make my point. You simply cannot think about some idea in a rational way and a faith-based way at the same time. They are nearly completely opposing modes of thought. And in order to make this point, the best place to start is probably with a couple of definitions. Nom nom nomenclature, ya know what I mean? Well if you do, then explain it to me, because I don't. In the meantime, here are some terms.

The first term is *religion*.

*Whoa! Hold on here, Mister! What's with all this religion talk? You told me we were going to discuss HOW TO THINK, yet here you are talking about religion instead of doing your job...are you trying to hustle me? Where's the thinking part?*

I'll get there, I promise. Because religion is the faith-based thinking with which I'm most intimately acquainted, it's going to be used frequently as a foil in this book. Because we need to make hats out of it to keep the government from listening to our thoughts. (I'm kidding, I'm kidding! Slow down, conspiracy theorists!) No, not that kind of foil...I'm talking about a *literary* foil. We're going to set the stage by introducing, and then critiquing, some irrational forms of thinking so we can demonstrate the need for more rational forms of thinking. But not everything about religion is irrational, so we need to pin down exactly what's being talked about here. Hence, the need to define it.

And on top of this, while my goal is to demonstrate that faith-based thinking is irrational, I need to point out that religion is not the only form of faith-based thinking in the world. Of course there are other forms of faith-based thinking. Religion does provide a powerful safe haven for faith-based thinking though, especially with regard to the (*cough* bandwagon fallacy *cough*).

With that said, the word *religion* is notoriously difficult to define. I kind of wonder if this is by design to some degree. If we can't define it, then we can't talk about it, and then it can't ever be scrutinized, you feel me? So let's give *religion* a definition so you know what I'm talking about. (I'm going to define it in two ways.) And I already accept from the outset that this is going to take defining some other words that might otherwise have vague meanings as well. But we're not going to get anywhere unless we start somewhere.

One of the best ways to define a word is to explain what I'm NOT talking about. (This creates a foil to the foil, and is necessary because it's like a 2-ply foil that keeps the alien

ESP out of our brains. Because alien ESP is much more powerful than government mind control. What were we discussing again? Oh yes, the parts of religion I'm NOT talking about.) Look, I get that religion can often be the source of a great community. So can the local Rotary club, or bridge night, or a hockey league. Community is NOT what I'm talking about, nor what I am critiquing with this book, except for the penchant of groups to fall prey to the (*cough* bandwagon fallacy *cough*). That's a bad cough I'm getting, I'm starting to think I need a throat lozenge or something. But if I only cough on the logical fallacies, I think I'll be alright. Let's see...where was I? (Maybe I need another layer of foil.) Also, did I mention the bandwagon fallacy already? Yep, there it is, right above.

Anyway, claiming something is true because "lots of people believe it" is a great argument, because *that many Mormons can't be wrong*. Did I get that bandwagon fallacy right, grandpa? (Yes, he seriously said this...and take it easy on my grandpa, your grandpa probably said the same thing about his religion.) I also get that there are parts of religions that are actually based on fact. Jerusalem is a real place. London is a real place too, so Harry Potter must be true, right? Is it factual that Jesus was a real person? He probably was, but regardless, if we're going to answer that kind of question in an evidence-based sort of way where we can all get on board, you're going to be looking at the question scientifically, not religiously. So no, I'm NOT talking about those historical elements of religion either. I also get that each religion does not put the same amount of stock in supernatural claims as every other religion, but supernatural claims *is* one of the things I'm talking about.

So for our purposes, I'm talking about two primary characteristic of religion:
   (1) Asserts supernatural claims (and thus, requires faith in those claims).
   (2) Requires loyalty, obedience, and zealotry to authority figures, which is often simply a byproduct of faith-based thinking.

If a religion has no faith in supernatural claims, nor an institutionalization of zealous obedience to authority, well then I guess, according to my definition, it's not a religion (*cough* No True Scotsman fallacy *cough*). I'm sorry, what's that? Oh you don't like this definition because it conveniently ignores examples that don't fit the point I'm trying to make? Okay, if you want to use a different word than religion, be my guest. But that's what I'm talking about when I use the term religion, and these are the elements of religion I'm critiquing.

"How dare you question faith?!" asks the person skeptical

of my statements about faith. Take a moment to think about the irony of that statement while I mention that I'm going to have a whole section of this book devoted to the definition of *faith* I'm using, and why elevating faith as a virtue is worthy of criticism. (That whole section is the next chapter.) A mind cannot entertain faith-based thoughts and skeptical thoughts at the same moment in time because they're two opposing modes of thought. Did you catch the irony above, by the way? I'll also devote a plethora of words to discussing my objections to obedience to authority. (Plethora...tenth grade English finally paid off. Score!) But we'll save that for another section as well.

Well darn it, I guess we're going to have to define *supernatural* as well. Why are we having to define this word too? This seems like a pretty self-explanatory word. Why? Because someone is going to complain about this later if I don't define it, that's why. For our purposes, I'm defining *supernatural* as "any proposed entity or force currently eluding objective, empirical measurement." And this is where my definition starts raising the hackles of those who want to believe in supernatural claims. How dare I, amirite? How dare I define something as "supernatural" just because we haven't discovered it yet? Does that mean atoms were supernatural at one point just because we couldn't measure them? *There are more things in heaven and earth than are dreamt of in your philosophy, Mr. Smarty Pants!*

And the answer to your question is YES, I'm saying that atoms were supernatural before they were objectively and empirically measured, according to my definition. So was Pluto. (Poor, poor demoted dwarf planet Pluto.) And so is Planet X, a celestial object hypothesized by Percival Lowell in the early 20th century (which likely doesn't exist). And so are little green men on Mars. Every hypothesized entity that hasn't been objectively and empirically measured, I'm calling supernatural.

And I was just about to define *irrational* right now, but I think maybe I'll define *rational* first. Rational is something that follows the rules of reason. Tah dah! That's it. Irrational doesn't follow the rules of reason. Pretty simple, huh? (*That sounds like a tautology, Mister. Unamused man is not amused*). The rules of reason are pretty well established. It may seem kind of unfair that they were established before you gave your input, and they didn't even consult you on what the rules should be. It may seem like I'm creating an arbitrary set of rules, and if your belief doesn't meet the criteria, then I'm just arbitrarily dismissing your belief. Let me tell you a little secret that the Science Bros aren't going to admit: there might be a teensy bit of truth to your critique. We'll get to this in a bit. Just hang tight. We're going to talk about the rules of reason, and I think you're going to agree that the rules of reason are pretty reasonable. But for now, let me define a rational explanation as "any explanation for an empirical measurement that follows established rules of logic." Are you okay with that? If not, you're going to have a bad time for a while. I truly am sorry. But that's the working definition for this book.

It's important to note that belief in a supernatural claim IS NOT rational. I'm going to spend a good portion of this book supporting this assertion, so hold your horses and keep reading. Belief in the supernatural is not rational. Because of this, you can't hold a supernatural belief AND think rationally at the same time. (*Still sounds pretty tautological, bud.*) But that's not to say that supernatural beliefs are the only irrational beliefs. Even though I said this before, I'm going to say it again: there are many other types of irrational beliefs. You got a hunch that you're going to win the lottery next week? That's also an irrational belief, and isn't necessarily a supernatural belief. So while I'll be using supernatural beliefs frequently as examples to contrast against rational belief, there are plenty of other irrational beliefs as well.

So now that we've defined *supernatural* and *rational*, and we've also contrasted them against one another, we need

How to Think 13

to get a nasty little secret of scientific thinking out of the way. In full disclosure, I need to tell you something very important, so please pay attention. It's possible that you believe in something currently classified as supernatural, and yet that belief might be entirely true. Science hasn't disproved leprechauns for example (*cough* it's not their job to *cough*), and they would be classified as supernatural at this time. According to established rules of logic, it is irrational to believe in leprechauns. But that doesn't automatically mean they don't exist. And so we need to hold a position philosophers call "epistemic humility". It's basically big words for philosophers to sound bigly. But it actually means something important. It means that we need to accept the fact that we don't know everything about the universe just because we've come up with some pretty clever rules we call logic.

I don't believe in leprechauns, but I also openly admit that I could be wrong about this lack of belief. Leprechauns may in fact exist, and we just don't have conclusive evidence for them that would meet the standards of logic and evidence. But what I hope to demonstrate by the end of this book is that the belief in leprechauns is still irrational nonetheless, the likelihood of leprechauns existing is really low, and if you consider yourself a reasonable, rational individual, you probably shouldn't believe in leprechauns. But at the very least, if you DO believe in leprechauns, I hope to convince you that you are not being rational AND believing *at the same moment* in your brain. Believing in leprechauns and thinking rationally are two *contradictory* mental processes. You can't eat your cake and have it too. Unless you barf it up. But it'd hardly be cake at that point would it? Where was I going with this? Oh look, a rainbow!

The complement to the possibility that you might be right about irrational beliefs is that you might be wrong about rational beliefs. Let's all say it together now:
*If something is irrational, that doesn't automatically make it false.*
*If something is rational, that doesn't automatically make it true.*
When something is rational, it's more likely to be true. But there are no guarantees in life. It is rational to believe in the existence of cows. I feel pretty confident in saying that I believe in cows. I was raised on a milk farm and milked cows by hand. I have a memory of many hours milking cows, getting kicked in the stomach by a cow hoof, getting head butt by a cow and landing face first in a pile of cow manure muck, and many other zany adventures centered on cows. I'm fairly confident cows exist. But epistemic humility demands that I admit I could be wrong about cows existing, as well as any other belief I'm fairly confident about.

Does this seem absurd to you that I would go to such lengths to admit I could be wrong about cows? Possibly, but in the spirit of the renowned physicist Richard Feynman (*cough* appeal to authority *cough*), I'm trying to "bend over backwards" to show how I might possibly be wrong about my position and how a faith-based thinker might be right. (Feynman's *Cargo Cult Science* talk is required reading. That's the talk where we read about "bending over backwards" to show how we might be wrong. Don't forget to read that talk. Simple search on the internet. Look it up and read it. Learn to "bend over backwards" to show how you might be wrong.) Anyway, there's a possibility that your supernatural belief might be right. But the *possibility* that you may be right still doesn't mean you're following the rules of logic to arrive at your beliefs. In any case, I hope you will also "bend over backwards" to show how you could be wrong about your own beliefs and your own mental processes. Can you do that? If not, we might have uncovered a major flaw in your way of thinking.

Alright, I'm going to get a little (*cough* slippery slope fallacy *cough*) to impress upon your mind the danger our world faces by NOT choosing, as a species, to adopt a more critical, rational, scientific mode of thinking. We need to discuss the urgency and need for more scientific, rational thinking in the world. If the world does not get more scientifically, rationally minded, in a very short space of time we could literally blow ourselves to smithereens! It could be the *end of the world!* With the advent of nuclear weapons, this is not mere hyperbole. There are some scientists who monitor what they call the "Doomsday Clock". It's currently set for 2 minutes to midnight, symbolically representing how close we are to humanity's imminent demise. This is based on a number of criteria, but essentially, it's how close we are to global thermal nuclear war, and the utter annihilation of humankind and life as we know it (Wouldn't you prefer a nice game of chess?). Two minutes to midnight! *Do you want to die*?! We need to start thinking more rationally! It is my assertion that the only way humanity can possibility reach this metaphorical midnight is through the irrational kind of thinking that I am critiquing in this book. And on the flip side, the only way we can save ourselves from this destruction is by utilizing the rational thinking that I am advocating in this book.

Okay, I'm going to guess that I have a lot of eyeballs rolling into the backs of heads from that last paragraph. Am I really arguing that religious-type thinking is going to lead to WWIII? Yes, that's exactly what I'm saying. But it can be a bit overwhelming to try to piece together how one's thinking can actually be harmful. You're a good person who would never hurt a fly. How could your faith-based thinking, something so fundamental to your being, be the greatest threat to humanity? I can see how hearing such news might make a person do whatever they can to expunge the information from one's brain and fight against it (*cough* cognitive dissonance *cough*). Because accepting such a proposition means that one's way of thinking is actually harmful for the world. The religious mode of thinking instantly tries to deflect such criticisms, either blocking them altogether or fighting against them. But rarely does it open itself to the possibility that it could be wrong. And this is another reason why such modes of thinking are not just different, but opposing and incompatible, to rational thinking.

Is this all a bit too heavy to think about right now? Even if we're taking a slightly less hyperbolic position, there are still many, many other ways in which religious thinking creates real harm in the world which doesn't necessarily blow up the entire planet. But I'm guessing such a list is going to cause a gag reflex as well. Nobody wants to hear that they're causing harm. Or that donations to religious organizations are being spent on harming others (giving money starts with thinking). The reaction of the religious mind will be to expunge such thoughts as well. Expunge...that's a really good word, I need to use it more frequently. Nearly every religious tradition ever invented has perpetuated harm upon women and minorities. *But I'm a woman and my church doesn't harm me!* Oh really? Tell me more about that... (*cough* Stockholm syndrome *cough*). Many of the major monotheistic religions have turned genital mutilation into an act of religious piety. Most attempts to insert unequal treatment under the law are introduced by, and supported through faith-based thinking. The Catholic church rocked the world with its child abuse scandal, yet the outrage just fizzled and died with nearly no change to the structure of the organization or removal of any sexual predators...er...I mean priests. The "holy" institution of supernatural faith and obedience to authority protected pedophiles. Over and again, women are told to keep quiet about abusive spouses and remain with those spouses. I know, because my mom was one of those women (*cough* anecdotal fallacy and appeal to emotion *cough*).

There are real problems in the world. The kind of problems that harm other people. And I'm often told by those asserting faith-based thinking that *religion isn't real the problem! Atheists kill people, too!* (*cough* tu quoque fallacy *cough*) *I mean, have you heard of Chairman Mao and Stalin? Or Pol Pot! So many more people have been killed by atheists than by religious people! And what about Hitler?* (*cough* whataboutism, which is the same fallacy as tu quoque *cough*). *Oh and while we're on the subject of Hitler...* (\*cough\* Gott mit Uns, look it up \*cough\*). *Okay, maybe not Hitler, but what about Mao and Stalin!*

In the words of Sam Harris, "The problem with fascism and communism, however, is not that they are too critical of religion; the problem is that they are too much like religions." Yes, Mao and Stalin might have fought specifically against supernatural thinking, but failed to get rid of unquestioning obedience and loyalty from their ideology. (Dang it, I missed an opportunity to use *expunge* again.) So while they might have been devoid of supernatural thinking, they were still strongly advocating a fanatical zealotry (i.e., fervent partisanship for a person, a cause, or an ideal) that mimics religious thinking. Zealotry, by definition, is NOT critical thinking about one's own cause or ideals. It actually requires that you not think critically about your own cause or ideals. And so it's antithetical to rational thinking. You cannot be a zealot and a rational thinker at the same moment in time. They are contradictory modes of thinking. And yes, there are lots of ways in which these modes of thought are contradictory...we're just getting started.

Are you willing to kill another person (i.e., someone who has no intention of killing you) for your ideals? If you are, you might be a zealot. Are you willing to use the law to harm other people in order to achieve your ideological aims? Then you might be a zealot. Most religious people I know personally would not consider themselves zealous in this regard. However, most religious people I know also adhere to one of the Abrahamic derived faiths and so they have this sort of zealotry codified in their religious texts. (Don't believe me? We'll get to this shortly.) If you are a follower of Abraham, you are not a true believer unless you're a zealot. Don't get mad at me about this. I didn't make the rules for your religion. Sorry. And yes, we'll cover this in the next chapter.

Let's take a step back for a moment so I can "bend over backwards" to validate your point about Mao and Stalin. In the meantime, can you also "bend over backwards" to validate mine? Yes, there are plenty of institutions that do not require belief in supernatural claims that are also incredibly dangerous for the world. They don't fit the traditional, common use of the word religion. But they do adhere to the second portion of my definition for religion: they require strict and unquestioning adherence to authority. (A fair and dictionary-supported definition of religious is zealotry, by the way.) Mao and Stalin produced the same zeal and fervor that often accompanies religious faith. But either way, I think we can agree what they are NOT doing is instilling critical thinking skills in their followers. Because these two modes of thought

How to Think 21

(uncritical obedience vs. questioning authority) are incompatible. You simply cannot hold both propositions in your mind at the same time. What I hope to convince you of is that we need less mindless obedience and more critical thinking in the world. And unfortunately, we cannot have both at the same time.

We all share the same physical world. People now have the power to utterly destroy the entire earth, and even laying that possibility aside, have the power to commit great atrocities on others. We need modes of thinking that help others, not harm others. In the long run, we all share the same fate. We don't have time to come up with some ecumenical, happy reconciliation with religious thinking. Religious thinking (belief in claims without evidence and zealous obedience) is the problem. We don't need to figure out how to accommodate the problem. We need to figure out how to fix the problem, and that fixing will come from changing the way humanity thinks.

Have I sufficiently explained the problem (the foil) of faith-based thinking that needs to be corrected by rational thinking? Actually, no, I haven't. I've only gotten started. There's still more to cover with regard to faith-based thinking. And we're going to take care of that in Chapter 2.

## Chapter 2 – What is Faith?

Alright, in order to answer this question, we're going to have to do some more defining. I recognize that we've spent a lot of time simply getting the meaning of words out of the way, but such an exercise on this topic is necessary and long overdue. We need to agree upon the meaning of words in order to convey the meaning of ideas. You don't like my definitions? Fine, but at least understand how I'm using the words so you follow what I'm talking about. Speaking of which, I think I should start an organization around my one and only true definitions for these words, where everyone just accepts my definitions on faith. And all who disagree with the meaning of these words as I have laid them out must be *expunged*! (I knew I'd find a way to get that word in again. And take it easy, I love you people, and I don't want anyone *expunged*. Yes, I used *expunged* again! And there again! I could do this all day.) But seriously, if you don't like my definitions, feel free to start up a debate with me, and tell me how you think I'm wrong. Argue rationally and I will listen to you. I like to "bend over backwards" to see how I might be wrong. But in the process, consider how you'd like me to be open to seeing how I might be wrong, and consider whether you'd give me (or anyone else) the same courtesy with your ideas. And if you aren't open to the possibility that you may be wrong, then consider the hypocrisy of your position, and the consistency of mine. Think how you can't be open and not open at the same time in the same brain. And recognize these are incompatible modes of thought. And good luck to ye, I love to debate.

As with some of the earlier definitions, let me start by explaining what I'm NOT talking about when I use the word *faith*. Often when people discuss the word *faith*, they are talking about many things all at once, and applying the benefits of one definition to other uses of the word, even though those benefits do not apply to all other meanings (*cough* equivocation fallacy). Some might accuse me of doing the reverse with the word *religion* in the earlier section. There might be some fair criticism there, but I've tried very hard to separate out the precise meanings that I am criticizing. Okay, to be fair, I didn't try that hard. I've been talking about these ideas for a very long time. The ideas flow pretty freely at this point. In any case, I think I've done a pretty good job of partitioning the meanings that are currently under criticism.

When I'm discussing faith here, I'm NOT criticizing self-confidence, the sort of thing that Disney movies sing about in many of their songs. Believe in yourself and you can do great things. Have faith in yourself. I totally agree with this. It's absolutely true that if you don't believe in yourself, you won't do great things. So you might as well have faith in yourself. To be fair, depending on how big the dream is, it's totally possible that it may be unreachable. Maybe you want to be an NBA basketball player and you're under 5 feet tall. There are hundreds of thousands of other people who have the same dream, and only so many spots available on the teams. If we're looking at things statistically (evidence-based), most people will not achieve their big dreams. But I don't care...statistics be damned...go out there and live that dream! Dream big, shoot for the stars, and make your dream come true. The purpose of this book is not to poo-poo your big dream. If you want to see those "glowing lanterns gleam," then go on and escape that tower (the one with that vaguely religion-inspired stepmom) and go for it. *You are good enough, smart enough, and people like you, Stuart!* If you need daily affirmations to keep going, then you keep telling yourself those words of positivity. I have zero qualms with that, and don't let me stop you. I'm not saying anything in this book to dissuade you from this. Believe in yourself, even if there's a certain amount of absurdity to that belief. Have I "bent over backwards" enough to make this point? I'm NOT talking about self-confidence when critiquing faith.

Another important point that needs to be made here is *WHY* I have to go to such great lengths to separate out these two types of "faith" (i.e., self-confidence vs. religious faith). Why is it so critical to make it perfectly clear that these are two very different types of activities? The answer is simple: because religion often ties your self-confidence to their supernatural claims. Religion entangles the two; I wish to disentangle them. I do not want your self-confidence harmed in any way by the words I'm sharing with you. In Mormonism – the religion I grew up in – this connection is made explicit in the Book of Moses (a book mimicking parts of Biblical Genesis, and "revealed" to Joseph Smith). In it, Moses is shown the cosmos, after which he concludes, "Man is nothing, which thing I never had supposed" (Moses 1:10). I have two takeaways from this very short phrase.

(1) First, Moses learns that humankind is worthless and/or nothing, and
(2) Second, the idea that he was worthless never entered into his mind until after the religious experience where he learned he was worthless.

Of course, any Mormon will tell you that my conclusions about this passage are way off, and they absolutely believe they do have worth. They have "infinite worth" because they are "children of God". And herein lies the entire crux of the problem. Your sense of self-worth, that wasn't even in question until you were told you are worthless, comes from the supernatural claims of the religion. Thus, if you stop believing in the claim, then ergo you are worthless. You didn't know that you were worthless until the religion told you were worthless, and now the self-worth and self-confidence you didn't know you needed is tied to the religious claim. The religion bestows validation upon you. It will grant you the highest of validations even. It will go so far as to grant you "cosmic significance", but only if you validate the "cosmic significance" of the religious institution as the grantor of your validation. (This paragraph wasn't entirely my own creation...unfortunately I've lost the source for this "cosmic significance" idea to give full credit.) Needless to say, this idea of making you feel worthless, then validating you through religious claims is not only a very cult-like tactic, but is also a very abusive spouse-like tactic. The very notion is the embodiment of emotionally abusive harm. It is the emotional equivalent of breaking your leg and then giving you a crutch that you didn't need in the first place. My personal sense of self-worth is not tied to any external force. I am good enough just because. You don't need external validation to love yourself. If anyone is telling you that you do, they are being abusive.

One last point on self-worth before we move on. Even though feeling like you're a "child of God" is not necessary to have self-worth and self-confidence (trust me, I know it's possible), once the emotional "leg" has been broken by religion and the crutch offered, faith may be a necessary support, even temporarily, to get some people through tough times. Religions are counting on that. They're counting on you having a lot of rough events in life and unable to get out of the pits of life without their help. Hmm, let's see if there's any analogy to this somewhere. Why yes, there is. It's sort of like when a person develops an alcohol dependency and requires the bottle to keep going. It's not healthy. It's not the best way to cope with tragedy or loss. But I recognize going cold turkey isn't always the best solution for many people.

In many ways, religious belief is like Dumbo's feather in this regard. The feather was never necessary for Dumbo's flight. (What's that? Yes, I get that the floppy ears weren't necessary either. Yes, yes, because elephants can't fly in the first place. Geez, we're getting pretty literal right now, aren't we? Just go with me for a minute. It's a good analogy.) The feather wasn't necessary for flight, but in a way, it was necessary. Even though it added no physical lift to raise him off the ground, it provided the emotional and psychological courage necessary to make the first leap. And here I'm "bending over backwards" to acknowledge that faith might be a temporary (yet necessary) support for some people psychologically. I try to go easy on people who are having a tough time in life. I'm not trying to pull the rug out from under people who legitimately need their faith to keep them hanging on. Faith might help people

feel better, but so do drugs. And they can both be
abused.

The world is in need of an intervention right now. This
book is one of those "come to Jesus" moments where we
should recognize that we need to stop coming to Jesus to
solve our problems. In all likelihood, Jesus isn't coming
back to save us from ourselves. (And even if he were
coming back, wouldn't he want us acting as good stewards
of the earth, making it better on our own anyway?) And
so for the sake of everyone else on the planet, do what you
can to wean yourself off of the sauce. (The "faith sauce"
that is. Was that not clear which sauce I was referring to?)

Alright, hopefully I have drawn a sufficient distinction
between what I'm definitely NOT talking about (which is
the legitimate source of self-confidence and self-worth)
versus what I AM about to talk about (which is the
following definition of *faith*...the one I am about to
critique). For our purposes, I'm defining faith as "a belief
held without sufficient evidence or even despite
contradictory evidence." Can we not see the problem with
faith based on that definition alone? Is it really necessary
to write an entire book to describe why this sort of mental
process is, by definition, irrational? Is it really necessary to
explain why you can't hold such a mental process and
think logically in the same brain at the same moment in

time?  Apparently so.  So let's continue.

In the Bible, the book of Hebrews defines faith as the "substance of things hoped for, the evidence of things not seen" (Hebrews 11:1).  This definition is wildly popular with many different Christian groups, and it also suffices for what I'm critiquing.  So it's fine to use this definition as well, since we're saying basically the same thing.  Faith is not evidence; it's a placeholder for the LACK of sufficient evidence to continue holding on to a belief (despite the lack of sufficient evidence).

Ringing in my ears at this very moment, I can hear the average Christian responding with, "*Ha ha! Gotcha! That's not what the Biblical verse means AT ALL! It's talking about evidence for things we can't see, just like anyone else requires faith when they don't have all the physical evidence.  Court cases convict criminals all the time even when no one was there to see the crime!  Gotcha, sucka!*" In other words, they're trying to say we all need to trust the evidence even if we don't have absolute certainty that the events happened exactly as we believe they did.  *And ha! Even if you don't believe in the Bible, you still have to "believe" some events happened a certain way too, Mr. Smarty Pants!  You have to believe something!  How did the universe get here?  You don't know with certainty, because you weren't there either!* And despite the levity,

I'm trying very hard to give an accurate representation of the likely retort to my explanation of the Biblical passage in order to avoid (*cough* straw man) misrepresentation. So again, if you feel I'm not quite capturing your understanding of the passage, then write me a letter. But I think I'm pretty close since I've heard this argument over and over.

Okay, while that interpretation of the Biblical passage certainly sounds better than just believing without evidence, it doesn't quite capture how many/most religious people actually use the term faith in practice. And here I am again "bending over backwards" to also acknowledge that court cases have to make certain assumptions based on the evidence. I grant this. We don't know with absolute, undeniable certainty that a person committed a crime, especially when there is no video evidence or eye witnesses, and even then that doesn't guarantee certainty. (Philosophically, there's no such thing as that absolute certainty anyway.) But this act of "making assumptions despite a lack of complete certainty" is something altogether different than faith. The logical assumptions used in a courtroom I would call *confidence*. And we should exhibit different levels of confidence based on different levels of evidence.

Now, this may seem entirely unfair that I'm pulling a new

word out of a hat (i.e., confidence) and using that term to distinguish between what happens in a courtroom and what religious people do when discussing gods, or universe creations, or resurrections, or partings of Red Seas and other such supernatural assertions. But here's why I feel totally justified doing so: if I were a judge, and the prosecution were trying to make their case, I would listen to the evidence. And if the argument were compelling based on the evidence and logic alone, then I would accept the assertion based on evidence and logic alone. When the evidence and logic are compelling enough on their own, we call that *Sufficient Evidence*. If the evidence and logic are not enough to make a compelling case, we call that *Insufficient Evidence*. But at no point is anyone arguing that sufficient evidence is the same thing as certainty.

But when I try to do the same exercise for religious/supernatural claims, the logic *always* ends up with a statement such as "just gotta have faith, man!" And now, gentle reader, do you see the difference? If the claim were simply reasonable enough based on evidence and logic alone, there would be NO NEED FOR FAITH. The prosecution in a trial does not, at any point, say, "just gotta have faith, jury!" Their job is to convince the jury based on evidence and logic alone. So within religious claims, faith is still the placeholder for the lack of *sufficient evidence*. Faith is the point where evidence and logic end, but you still need a little something extra (or a lot something extra) to get you from the evidence and logic to belief.

And the religious position is actually even worse than I've demonstrated so far. When I ask a religious person for evidence of cows, I have never, ever heard someone say, "just gotta have faith, man!" They just provide the evidence for cows without ever invoking the concept of faith. When there is a religious lawyer presenting a case, they never, ever tell the judge "just gotta have faith, your honor!" Even the religious lawyer knows there's a certain amount of absurdity packed into that statement. In every other domain beyond their religious belief, the religious person just presents *Sufficient Evidence*. Where there is sufficient evidence, no religious person invokes the term "faith", except to befuddle the discussion with a non-analogous court case scenario (*cough* equivocation fallacy). And so I feel pretty good using the definition of faith as I have laid it out, and contrasting that with *confidence* which is an altogether different concept.
*Confidence is belief based on sufficient evidence.*
*Faith is belief despite insufficient evidence.*

And with that definition in place, let's now delve into the truly unfortunate and harmful nature of faith. This will likely be the toughest part of the entire book for religious people to read. But it's absolutely essential to understand this to understand the nature of faith. I've discussed this idea at length with many highly intelligent religious friends, and the universal response is one of almost complete denial of the obvious conclusion I'm drawing here. So I apologize in advance for the (*cough* cognitive dissonance) that is likely about to take place, and I won't be surprised if you feel like I'm totally wrong in my conclusion. Of course, if your response is like every other conversation I've had around this subject, you won't be able to tell me *WHY* I'm wrong. You'll just be able to tell me over and over again *THAT* I'm wrong. In other words, you will hold a conviction in your mind for which there is *insufficient evidence* but hold it nonetheless. In other words, you will believe I am wrong because of faith, not because of evidence, and further demonstrate that religious thinking and rational thinking cannot exist in the same mind at the same time.

Alright, here we go. I'm going to tell you two stories using the same characters, the same setting, the same major plot points, but with one singular difference. And that one singular difference is *faith*. The two stories are both about Abraham, his son Isaac, and God Almighty. The setting is a sheep pasture. And if you can picture me as a cowboy telling the story around a campfire, that might help. I don't know why…I just like telling stories with a cowboy accent. Anyway, here's what happens:

(1) In the first tellin' of this here story, Abraham and Isaac are working all day with their sheep in the sheep pasture in the hot sun. Woo wee! Abraham is in truth hot and thirsty when he gets home that afternoon after slaving away in the pasture with his son, Isaac, taking care of those sheep. From exertion and dehydration, that man is parched! Logic and reason, and past experience, tell Abraham to grab himself a nice cold drink out of yonder creek, and so he wipes the sweat from his brow and starts meandering down to the source of water. Being the good father that he is, he also decides he will fill up his sheep bladder flask with water for his son Isaac as well. Just then, God Almighty appears before Abraham. Abraham is shocked! He falls to the earth, partially because of the dehydration, and posits, "What dost thou require of thy servant, dear LORD?" God Almighty responds, "Abraham, my faithful servant, I command you to get a drink of water for thyself and thy son, who is also certainly great with thirst as well." Abraham looks stupefied at God Almighty for a moment, then nods and does that little click with his tongue while he points both

index fingers and says, "You got it, God! I was just fixin' to do that anyway!"

(2) In the second tellin' of the story, Abraham and Isaac are working in the pasture with the sheep. Yada yada yada. It's super-duper hot; they're thirsty and head home. Wiping the sweat and all that. On the way to yonder creek, same exact event happens...God Almighty appears to Abraham. And just as before, Abraham falls to the ground, possibly because of dehydration. "What dost thou require?" and all that. God Almighty responds, "Abraham, I want you to take your son Isaac up to the top of yonder Moriah Mountain and kill him." Abraham gets ready to do the tongue click thing and the finger point thing and then stops in his tracks. "Um, what did you say?"

There is literally only one plot point difference between these stories. In the first story, Abraham is exhibiting precisely zero faith even though he's doing exactly what God Almighty commanded him to do (lay aside the "God Almighty appearing" thing for the time being, since that could have been as a result of his dehydration anyway). And the reason the first story requires zero faith is simple: Abraham doesn't need to exhibit faith to follow the command to get a drink of water, because logic, rationality, and most of all, thirst have already convinced him to go to the creek and get a drink of water anyway. A history of drinking water to quench thirst is *Sufficient Evidence* for believing drinking water will quench his thirst. There is no faith involved because evidence and logic supply all necessary justification for the act. There is no room for faith, and there would be no point for invoking faith in this scenario at all. He doesn't need to have faith in God Almighty's command because that's what logic and bodily need were driving him to do anyway.

In the second story, Abraham's famous response to this story requires an immense amount of faith (in case you missed the memo, Abraham actually agreed to this madness in the Biblical account). In many Abrahamic traditions, this story of Abraham's willingness to slay his only son is not simply an example of great faith, but held up as the supreme pinnacle of faithful expression. No greater faith can be displayed than the willingness to kill your own child. But why is there such a division between the two stories? The stories are nearly identical except for the command to Abraham. And any Bible believing person could tell you the difference. Because getting a drink of water when you're thirsty is totally logical and rational, and killing your own kid (or even the willingness to do so) is BATSHIT CRAZY! And it's not just a little bit batshit crazy. It's the supreme pinnacle of batshit crazy.

When God Almighty commands something entirely reasonable and rational, it requires zero faith. When God Almighty commands something entirely unreasonable (nay even the supreme pinnacle of unreasonable), it requires the most faith. If God Almighty had commanded something that was somewhat absurd (let's say approximately halfway between completely reasonable and batshit crazy) it would require approximately half of the faith of killing your only kid.

At this point, Can you see the glaring problem with faith? If not, think of this problem in terms of a two-dimensional graph, where we put "faith" on the horizontal axis and "illogical" on the vertical axis. If we were to plot out the various possible commands God Almighty could have possibly given to Abraham, they all draw a 45-degree line running diagonally up the graph. The command to drink water would be 0% illogical, and so it would fall on the 0 of the vertical (illogical) axis. It would also require the least amount of faith (zero faith to be exact), and so would fall on the 0 of the horizontal (faith) axis as well. The command to kill his kid is the most illogical act a human can perform, and so would fall on the highest point of the vertical (illogical) axis. It would also require the highest pinnacle of faith, and so would fall on the highest point of the horizontal (faith) axis.

# How to Think 39

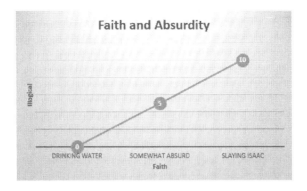

There is a one-to-one correspondence between that which requires faith and that which is illogical. This is true in every situation, not just Abraham's. If killing your kid could be justified logically, it wouldn't require faith. But because of the off-the-charts level of absurdity of the act, it's held up as the pinnacle of faith. Are you catching this? Faith *is* absurdity. They are equivalent. Think about this. Go back and read this whole section again if you need to. It is only when the absurd is invoked that faith is invoked. Again, we don't invoke "just have faith, bro" in a court case, because the attorney doing so would be laughed out of the courtroom. Faith as a rationale only flies where people are willing to accept the absurd as an explanation. Because they have a 1:1 correspondence. You can't have it both ways. You can't say that an assertion lacks logical support, but then call it logical, because it is de facto illogical. If it has logical support, then you just give the logical support. Everybody does this (*cough*

bandwagon fallacy, I know). And if an assertion has logical support, then there's no need to invoke faith. Unfortunately, any claim requiring "faith" as its support is not logical. And so, as unfortunate as it is, faith and reason cannot be held in the same mind at the same time. They're not merely *different* modes of thinking. They are *contradictory and incompatible.*

At this point, one of the next fronts the intelligent religious person falls back to is the one proposed by Stephen Jay Gould, that science and religion represent "Non-overlapping magisteria." The argument goes something like this: science is only concerned with physical, empirical facts about the universe, and religion is only concerned about values. And so they never actually cross paths. So of course you can hold them in your mind at the same time, because faith and science are never used to address the same questions. *Yeah! This explanation sounds good, doesn't it! It supports my preconceived notion that I can hold them both in my mind at the same time* (\*cough\* confirmation bias). *So even if all that unintelligible 1:1 correspondence between faith and absurdity is true (and no one's agreeing it is true, Mr. Smarty Pants, even if we can't tell you why it's not true), it doesn't even matter anyway. I can be a little absurd about the source of my values, right? Values aren't subject to scientific inquiry anyway. So we CAN hold faith and science in the same* *brain at the same time! Boom! Gotcha, sucka!*

Well, that sounds just great. And we could end the discussion right there except that there are a few problems with the argument. (Actually, more like the entire argument.) First of all, they DO overlap. Unless religion wants to get completely out of the business of making claims about objective reality, they will always overlap. For example, what is the age of the universe? While I'm assuming the number of Young Earth Creationists are steadily decreasing in the face of scientific evidence, at least a small percentage of the population still takes it on religious faith that the universe is only 6,000 or so years old. (Some people may only claim this about the earth rather than the entire universe. Don't get super caught up in the details; it's the same problem.) In any case, our best scientific estimation is around 13.799 billion years. There are many, many empirical bases for this estimation, and they all converge right around the same point in time. Those advocating a 6,000 year old universe are not anywhere remotely close to the scientific estimation.

Again, it needs to be noted that you can't hold these two ideas in your head at the same time. Both can't be right, and your brain can only accept one or the other, not both. If you hold to the faithful timeline, you must reject the scientific explanation (and thus much of how science understands the universe) or you reject the religious claim. In other words, you must believe the absurd despite the evidence to the contrary. Or in other words, you must have faith. The alternative is to let go of the religious claim, and choose to accept the rational perspective. But regardless of which assertion you accept, BOTH assertions are being made about the same objective, empirical thing: the age of the universe. These are not "non-overlapping magisteria". They couldn't be more perfectly overlapping.

That's just one example, but there are a never-ending supply of claims made by religion about the objective, empirical world. Did Moses's staff objectively, empirically turn into a snake in Pharaoh's court? Was Moses even a real person? Did Joseph Smith have physical gold plates? Could he legitimately translate ancient Egyptian from the papyri he purchased? Did Jesus actually physically resurrect? Was there a man named Jesus at all? Did Moses part the Red Sea and was the actual Pharaoh of Egypt drowned in the waters? We may not have the ability to answer these questions from a practical perspective (simply because we may not have the means to answer them), but that doesn't mean they aren't scientific questions. (Actually, we can pretty easily answer whether Joseph Smith could translate Egyptian text. Spoiler alert! He couldn't. Some of the other questions are a bit more difficult to pin down with as much confidence.) Every question I've listed here are religious claims made about the empirical, physical world and are thus within the realm of science. And so they're religious claims that overlap with science. This happens all the time. If someone claims aliens abducted them and took them into their spaceship, this again is an empirical, physical claim, though it could also legitimately be classified as a faith-based claim.

Yes, religions could get completely out of the empirical claim business and change all of their empirical claims to "metaphors" (which is a growing trend actually), but what is religion at that point? Does it matter at all if the empirical claims are actually true? For example, many Abrahamic traditions believe that you have a "soul" that continues on after you die. Does it matter at all whether this claim actually represents the true state of reality, or is it okay if such claims are simply "metaphors"? i.e., when you die you're no longer there in actuality, but you're still there as a "metaphor"? Are you okay with it just the same either way? Does it matter at all if Abraham really received a revelation from God Almighty to kill his son or that he might have been delusional from his dehydration? Would that make any difference at all? If it does matter, then we cannot escape the fact that there is a tension of sorts between religious claims that spill into the empirical, physical world and the ability of science to investigate those claims.  And where the claims conflict, you cannot hold both propositions concurrently.

So religious claims do spill into the empirical world all the time.  But also, science can absolutely spill into the world of values.  We absolutely can look at values under the microscope of science as it were, and make good decisions related to the values we choose as individuals and societies.  I would highly recommend Sam Harris's book *The Moral Landscape* with respect to this question.  He was criticized for not bearing his burden of proof for demonstrating truly objective values.  I have the highest respect for the book, but from a purely philosophical stance, I agree with the criticisms.

But that's hardly the point.  Religions have NEVER demonstrated that they have truly objective values.  So what?  We have many shared values nonetheless (*cough* bandwagon fallacy, I know).  Given the common goals of desired outcomes, we can absolutely measure the cause-and-effect of certain values in achieving those outcomes.  For example, if we have the desired outcome of not being murdered, we can absolutely measure the effect of different values (such as increased gun control) on achieving that goal.  We can do this scientifically.  This ain't rocket science.  But it's still science.  Gould's claim that the two domains are non-overlapping is simply false.

And now, gentle reader, I will change gears at this juncture to make a slightly different kind of comparison between religious thinking and scientific thinking. Up to this point, I've been contrasting them as being antithetical, but there are some regards in which they are similar. As already mentioned, Gould's claim of non-overlapping domains is false. They definitely overlap and both attempt to answer empirical questions about the universe. In fact, it might be argued that they even start out on similar paths for this exact reason. For example, there is a natural land bridge between India and Sri Lanka. Of course, geology has an explanation for how that land bridge got there. I don't know what that explanation is, but I can almost guarantee two facts: first, that the world of science has already asked and come up with a plausible answer for that question; and second, that the answer isn't supernatural. However, Hinduism ALSO has an answer for how that land bridge got there. And wouldn't you know it, the answer *is* supernatural. The god Rama built the bridge supernaturally in order to save his goddess wife Sita from the Demon King living in Sri Lanka.

As I've mentioned several times already, both of those answers can't be correct. However, the paths to arrive at the explanations both share some commonalities. The first step of both paths is that humans noticed the land bridge there and began to wonder about it. Whether you are a Hindu who believes the story of Rama and Sita literally, or a geologist studying it, you had to start by noticing the formation that was there. The second step for both paths is that humans are filled with wonder about the origin of the bridge, and as a consequence, create a hypothesis about its origin. From this point, the paths of science and faith diverge, but for that short space of time, they run parallel along these two points. And where they diverge is the entire difference between religious faith and scientific reasoning.

We're going to spent much of the remainder of the book talking about the divergent paths each of these worldviews take and why they are incompatible. But the key point to garner from this example is that the wonder and hypothesizing of religious faith stops here. Once the hypothesis is formed, if you doubt the claim, you are no longer exhibiting religious faith. On the path of science though, this is merely the beginning of the journey. The hypothesis is just something to get the scientist started, and the instant response to your own hypothesis should be to attempt to prove it wrong. So while they start out looking very similar, what is considered "good religion" is actually "really bad science." And what is "good science" is actually "really bad religion". Religion may eventually change its tune on the original hypothesis. But the act of clinging to the hypothesis over thousands of years is simply NOT the path of science. If you take one path, philosophically you are de facto giving up the other path. There is no alternative, because clinging to the original hypothesis with the eyes of faith cannot take place if you instantly question (and try to disprove) the hypothesis. So while they may start out on similar paths, in order to "do science" you must "not do faith" and vice versa. Because they are diametrically opposed in this regard. As well as all the other ways we've already discussed. And all the other ways we're about to discuss.

This was a rather large chapter, so let's recap the highlights:
- I'm NOT criticizing self-confidence or believing in yourself.
    - It's okay to dream big.
- Your self-worth does not come from your religious belief, and it is okay to disentangle the two.
- Confidence and faith aren't the same thing.
    - Confidence is belief based on sufficient evidence.
    - Faith is belief despite insufficient evidence.
- Faith has a 1:1 correspondence to absurdity.
- Faith-based claims spill into the empirical world all the time, and can thus be tested empirically.

# Chapter 3 – The Foundation of Science

Well, here we are at chapter three. I don't know exactly what it is about chapter threes, but I really like them. Let's just take a minute to congratulate ourselves on getting to this point, shall we? Even though I'm having a fabulous time writing this, it's still a lot of work. So I'm going to pat myself on the back for making it here. I mean, normally when you get to a chapter two, that's somewhat of an accomplishment, but not really what I would consider "let's go out to TGI Fridays to celebrate" kind of an accomplishment. It's nothing like when you make it to chapter three. And you, gentle reader, should congratulate yourself too, especially if you're a religious person reading all about why faith-based thinking is not only irrational, but harmful to the world.

Yep, we talked quite a bit about the words *faith* and *supernatural* and why belief in them is equivalent to irrationality. We also talked about why zealous obedience, which derives from faith-based thinking, is one of the greatest dangers (if not the greatest danger) to humanity. In other words, the first two chapters were a criticism of how NOT to think. If that's all this book did and we stopped there, then that'd be quite a bit of a bait-and-switch now wouldn't it? Especially since the book isn't called *How NOT to think*. So I think it's only fair that we should now spend some time on HOW TO THINK, don't you think? I criticized faith-based thinking in the previous chapters (and I guarantee I'll do it again before we're finished). But that's not an entirely helpful exercise unless I replace the less-effective method of thinking with a more effective method of thinking. I've stated that faith-based thinking is de facto irrational. But what exactly constitutes rational thinking? That question is the topic under consideration starting now.

Much earlier in the book, I defined *rational* as "something that follows the rules of reason" (\*still sounds a lot like a tautology\*). That wasn't very thorough of me, and it may have felt somewhat like a cop out at the time. And to a small degree it probably was. But only because the train was headed in the opposite direction in the earlier chapters. But even though it might have been a cop out at the time, I did promise that I'd return to the topic. The time to return to that topic is now.

If you recall (and even if you don't recall) I gave the word *rational* a slightly longer definition as well: "any explanation for an empirical measurement that follows established rules of logic." That's a pretty good definition if I do say so myself. Well, actually, it may be longer, but unless we clarify some things, it's not any better than the first definition. There are a few potential problems here. Let's start with the problem that may be the least obvious. This is me "bending over backwards" to point out that the word *established* is kind of a fallacy (*appeal to tradition*). Just because the rules are established, that doesn't make them automatically right. "Because mama says so" doesn't quite cut it logically, though I'm sure it was fine in mama's house. We'll try to take it to the next level here, no disrespect to mama.

So in order to make my case, I need to support the assertion that the rules of logic really are reasonable, not just state that they're "established" and leave it at that. I will do precisely this in the current chapter as well as continue to explore the topic in the next. And for the second potential problem, why does rationality only pertain to "empirical measurement"? That sounds like an obvious (*No True Scotsman fallacy*). Are you telling me that just because I can't measure God or angels or leprechauns, it's irrational to believe in them? Just because there's nothing there to measure? Eh, kind of. But let's save that one for a bit. I promise we will discuss this question fully in this chapter. Because this is chapter three! Chapter three is going to be awesome! Because it's chapter three! (*circular reasoning, but it's just a joke...ease up a little*).

Yep, chapter three. So great! (*Looks around the room with hope and vigor...but then remembers what we're up against in chapter three.*) Oh, wait...uh oh...chapter three. Argh. That reminds me. Remember when we were talking about Abraham and how his willingness to kill his own kid was the most batshit crazy thing a person could possibly do, and remember I had mentioned that it was probably going to be the toughest thing a religious person would have to read in the entire book? And remember how I said it was smooth sailing and all downhill from there? Well, okay...yeah. Chapter three isn't so much of an affront to cherished religious beliefs and traditions as it is some relatively difficult concepts to grasp. Wait! Don't go anywhere! It's not that difficult. Stick with me, I promise it'll be worth it if you put in the effort to wrap your mind around them. Just remember, Jesus said, "I never said it would be easy; I only said it would be worth it" (*actually he never said that*).

If you look up *rational* in the dictionary, it gives you, not so much a definition, but more of a list of synonyms. Even the definition is generally something like "in accordance with reason or logic". But if you don't know what *rational* means, how are looking up *reason* or *logic* going to help, since their definitions more or less point back to *rational*? One of the synonyms for *rational* is *common-sense*, but that's the whole problem here, isn't it? Faith-based thinking is a sort of "sense" that many people commonly rely on...it's an incredibly common form of thinking actually. But that doesn't make it rational. That just makes it (*bandwagon fallacy*). By that definition, faith-based thinking may be common-sense, but faith-based thinking also isn't rational. So to what shall we appeal for an understanding of rationality?

Instead of just "taking it on faith" that the "established rules of logic" are reliable, let's follow the same historical path that got us to now and investigate how and why the decisions were made to call one thing rational and another thing irrational. In order to do this, we're going to need to get on a "magic school bus" of sorts...the kind that only exists in your imagination!...imagination...echo!...echo! In this magic bus, we can travel to any point in history. So let's go back to the furthest time you can think of. Were you thinking of the Old West? I was, but only partially because I could really go for a sarsaparilla right now. I'm parched! But that's actually not far enough back in time. How about King Tut? Getting warmer, but not nearly far enough. Although if you were thinking of ancient Egypt, I'm giving you that slow-nodding smile right now. You know what I'm talking about, right? No, no! Not the creepy kind from across the room at the bar. More like the "I've found a kindred spirit" kind of nod. I love ancient Egypt. But that's still not far back enough. Were you thinking of hundreds of millions of years ago, like dinosaur times? Much better, and we'll come back to this. But no.

I'm thinking even further back than the dinosaurs. More like 4 billion-ish years ago, the Hadean period, at the advent of the very first microorganisms on the planet. Okay, we're back far enough now. I bet you were thinking about the abiogenesis (i.e., how life began), weren't you? If you were, I can tell you're a real thinker and you were very close, but that's actually not quite where I was going with this. Your magic school bus overshot our destination by maybe a couple hundred million years. (It's a good topic for thinking about, no doubt. And maybe we'll cover it later. Not now.)

For now, I want to look at two traits that must have certainly formed in these earliest single-cell organisms: The first is the trait to move TOWARD food and the second is to move AWAY from danger. At some point along the evolutionary process, these lil' guys picked up the ability to move and the ability to sense their surroundings, and through that sensory perception, could distinguish food from foe. And most importantly to my point, they got it right. And how do I know they got it right? Well, the ones who didn't get it right ended up being food for the ones who did get it right. Or they ended up starving rather than surviving. With their little input processing systems rather than brains, it's certainly possible that random chance gave them a set of circuits that got it exactly wrong, i.e. I guess it's possible they were programmed to move toward danger and away from food, yet somehow continued to survive through their descendants for billions of years. Certainly it's possible that those organisms, and even all of their posterity down until the present day (including humans), have simply stumbled upon food and escaped foes by dumb luck. Yes, if I must "bend over backwards" to acknowledge this incredibly unlikely possibility, I will gladly do so. But probably much more likely some of those microorganisms just randomly developed accurate "logic gates" that correctly interfaced with their environments and that helped them survive. And then they passed those traits on to their posterity. Even if this trait was bestowed randomly initially, eventually all (or nearly all) of the organisms who didn't have the trait died off due to their inability to correctly MEASURE the danger and food around themselves.

And in a very real sense, we are the recipients of those magnificent traits first acquired 4 billion-ish years ago. They are a subset of a collection of traits that I will now call *rationality*, or in other words, "the ability to correctly measure reality as it really is." What?! Certainly I can't be trying to say that a microbe is rational, can I? Yes, in their own little way, microorganisms are "rational". In their own little way, computer circuits are rational, too, because they can correctly process reality-based information given to them as input. When we say an explanation is "reasonable", what we are really saying is that the explanation is supported by empirical measurement. Don't believe it? Well, stick with me. This is important. When someone bumps their head, the first thing we check is whether they still have their wits about them. And how do we check that? We hold up a certain number of fingers and ask, "How many fingers am I holding up?" It is the agreement upon the objective, empirical number of fingers that determines whether the wits are there or not. Even if they took a big bump on the noggin, they are still reasonable and rational if they can correctly measure the world about them.

Not every mental process is an exercise in rationality. When the mind is conceiving ideas that aren't measuring reality correctly, we'll call it *imagination*. And look, imagination is an important skill as well. But imagination is not rational unless it ALSO correctly measures reality. Ideas conceived of in the imagination, but that have no measurable correspondence to the real world, are fiction. There is no rational reason for believing in such ideas, by definition (*tautology, but this is my whole point*). And so such a belief is irrational. I guarantee if the day ever comes where we can measure leprechauns, scientists would believe in them. There's no secret conspiracy of scientists trying to keep the world from believing in leprechauns. Or is there? (*relax illuminati chasers, no seriously relax*).

So rationality is fundamentally the ability to correctly deduce cause-and-effect through MEASUREMENT. In other words, it's the ability to give correct explanations for empirical measurements. The input of rationality is MEASUREMENT. The output is CORRECT EXPLANATION. When they are in alignment, the explanation is reasonable. When they are out of alignment, the explanation is unreasonable. But the goal of rationality is to measure reality. Explanations that are not based upon any sort of measurement are unreasonable. Are we cool on this point? This is important.

Okay, if we're good on this point, let's hop back into our magic school bus and travel to the time of dinosaurs. Here we see the same trait as was in the microorganisms. Yes, dinosaurs were rational in their own little, er, big way too. The T-Rexes who could correctly move toward food and away from danger survived and passed their genes onto their chicken descendants. Hey, easy! Having a chicken as a grandkid is nothing to be ashamed of! Chickens are delicious!

Microorganisms and dinosaurs are cool, but let's jump back into the magic school bus and get back to the time of humans. Right about 400BC in China. When a guy named Sunzi lived (probably) and wrote a little book called the *Art of War*. In that book, he came up with some powerful concepts that are still used by military strategists today, as well as business executives and any other students of strategy. In chapter four of his book, he taught that winning wars (or any conflict) is dependent upon strategy, but strategy is dependent upon calculation, and calculation is dependent upon measurement of true conditions of the earth, or in other words, the true conditions of reality. And then in chapter 13, he explains that the only way to know the conditions of the enemy is by looking at them, via the use of spies. He even contrasts his incredibly practical approach to discernment through supernatural means by explicitly stating that you cannot learn about the enemy's position and plans by appealing to spirits. He figured this out 2,400 years ago. If you want to know what's going on, you LOOK. And if anyone doubts the effectiveness of Sunzi's tactics, I will happily challenge you to a contest where some random objects are left in a room. You use a "supernatural" means to discover the contents of the room, and I'll just look. I think just about anyone would bet on my chances. Because most anyone can see the absurdity of relying on supernatural means vs. looking. And in case you're wondering, no I did not bring up Sunzi just to plug my book, *Understanding the Art of War*, available on Amazon.com (\*shameless plug\*). Reasonable strategy of any kind is based on empirical measurement of reality. Did I mention that Sunzi understood this in 400BC?

When a lab rat presses the red button to get a treat, it's using rationality to make that decision. It is basing its button-pressing actions (with those cute widdle paws) on supportable reasons. It is reasonable because it has learned the true nature of cause-and-effect between the button and the treat.

Ironically, there was a famous experiment by B. F. Skinner where pigeons were given food, not by pressing the red button, but at entirely random intervals. In other words, the birds' actions had no effect whatsoever on the timing of the food distribution. But the birds appeared to believe that their actions had some effect, just like the rats and the red button. They seemed to build up a superstition of sorts around their actions and the dispensing of the food. There is certainly disagreement about what the birds were actually doing, but what isn't in question is that humans definitely do this. An action is considered superstitious (and therefore unreasonable) because there is no correlation between cause (e.g. rubbing a lucky rabbit's foot) and effect (good luck?). It is irrational to think there is a cause-and-effect relationship where there isn't. But the difference all boils down to MEASUREMENT.

Of course, religious people take measurement of the empirical world and also use those measurements as evidence of their faith-based claims. They do this all the time. On a rainy day, the sun came out right when you started giving your speech. Therefore, God has approved of your undertaking. Obviously, right? We are pattern-seeking creatures. We want to make sense of the world around us. Why do we do this? It probably has nothing to do with 4 billion-ish years of evolution. Must be some other reason. (*maybe some people aren't catching my sarcasm in this paragraph, so let me point it out*).

Anyway, we all look for patterns. Superstition is finding patterns where there aren't patterns. Science is finding patterns where there are patterns. So the only real difference between superstition and science is STATISTICS. Science is merely counting the hits and misses and seeing if your theory lines up enough to accurately describe reality. Faith-based thinking sees a pattern that isn't really a pattern and clings to the interpretation of the data and, following *Journey*'s advice, never stops believing. Science sees a pattern, forms a hypothesis, and then does everything it can to try to disprove the interpretation of the data. You cannot do both of these things at the same time. They are contradictory, incompatible modes of thinking about the data. (By the way, are you seeing a pattern where I'm demonstrating all of the ways these contradictory modes of thought can't occur in the same person at the same time?) So everyone is looking for patterns. If you see patterns, but you're afraid to count your hits and misses, you might be superstitious. If you see patterns, but you're NOT afraid to count your hits and misses, then you might be scientific. But you can't be both at the same time.

On our previous stop of the magic school bus, we were around 400BC in China. Close to that same time in Greece there was this little known philosopher named Aristotle, who shaped most of the thinking in the Western hemisphere for the next 2,000 years or so. You might have heard of him. He had a lot of great ideas about logic, and a few not so great ideas. He wrote everything down and gave it to Leia Organa to keep away from the evil Empire. Sorry, I'm being told that's not true. His writings were collected by his followers into a work called *The Organon*. One of the concepts in that work that he was very famous for was codifying the principles of deductive reasoning through the use of syllogisms. Basically that's a really fancy way of saying that he thought he could draw true truths from axiomatic premises (*and he was totally not begging the question*). In other words, you don't need to measure reality to learn truths, you can draw truth directly from your mind. To be fair to Aristotle, I'm greatly oversimplifying, and he did recognize that there was some benefit to inductive reasoning (i.e., measuring reality), but it was mostly to prime the mind's *intuition* in order to allow intuition to find the real truths. In other words, real science began with intuition. Wow, that sort of flies in the face of everything I've been saying for the last little bit about MEASUREMENT and whatnot. Anyway, we should probably look at what he said because maybe I've been wrong all this time. Let's look at what Aristotle had going here with his syllogisms. If you don't remember syllogisms from your college philosophy class, the really famous one goes like this:

> Premise 1: All men are mortal.
> Premise 2: Socrates is a man.
> Conclusion: Therefore, Socrates is mortal.

Totally makes sense, and it's totally rational, right? Aristotle was da man. Wow! Pure logic with no appeal to anything empirical. Damn, Aristotle, lay down those sick premises about men being mortal and Socrates being a man, and you have a totally legit undeniable, irrefutable conclusion. Deductive logic. Empiricism isn't even necessary. It's where truth is at. I guess this is why I know my cat has laser eyes...um...wait...what the what? Yes, my cat has effing laser eyes! Don't believe me? Here, I'll show you! Using DEDUCTION!

> Premise 1: All cats have laser eyes
> Premise 2: My cat, Petunia, is a cat.
> Conclusion: Therefore, my cat Petunia has laser eyes.

Same exact structure as the famous syllogism, so it must be true! We proved it deductively! Hmm, maybe something isn't quite right here. I guess deductive reasoning might have an inherent flaw, which is that it's still dependent that the premises are true. And how do we check whether the premises are true? We do it by empirical MEASUREMENT of reality. (i.e., we do it by INDUCTION.) It's like you can't escape this stuff if you try.

Anyway, that was a real nice stop in history. Thanks for that awesome lesson in deductive logic, Aristotle. That'll really help us avoid empirical measurement. And did I mention my cat has laser eyes?

Before we continue on with our European tour, let's take a quick stop in the Islamic Golden Age, around the 11$^{th}$ century, to visit a couple of scientific hipsters...they were doing science at least 500 years before it was cool in Europe. The first is Ibn al-Haytham (Alhazen) who argued that hypotheses need to be confirmed by repeatable experimentation, rather than intuition. He even called into question a long-held theory supported by Aristotle, Ptolemy, and Euclid that vision worked like headlights (i.e., our eyes provided the light to see). He upended the theory by repeated experimentation as well as demonstrating "eye lights" were simply unnecessary.

Alhazen's contemporary Ibn Sina (Avicenna) also understood the problems of Aristotle's beliefs concerning induction. In addition, he pointed out the power of experimentation and relying on measurement to tell us about reality. Many of the works of both Ibn al-Haytham and Ibn Sina were translated and studied in medieval Europe. Ibn Sina's medical works were studied for hundreds of years, for example. But the insight they had discovered regarding experimentation and empiricism didn't catch on in Europe for many hundreds of years later. It was almost like Ibn Sina was waving his hand in front of his face shouting, "You can't see me!" but then reminded everyone of the importance of "hustle, loyalty, and respect." Wait, that was John Cena.

Okay, back in the bus and let's head to the early 17th century to visit one of the most salty, delicious men ever to walk the earth, Sir Francis Bacon. Kevin lived about 2,000 years after Aristotle and pretty much everyone at that time (in Europe at least) still thought like Aristotle, i.e., that you could pull premises out of your arse and then deduce indisputable conclusions from rational thought. Like the *real* truth. Truth started in the mind, and as long as you thought about it long enough and hard enough, the conclusion must be true (*please catch that I'm being sarcastic here*). Anyway, Sir Francis was almost as thrilled by deductive reasoning as I am, but wondered why his cat didn't have laser eyes when Aristotle promised him the proof was right there in the syllogism. All he wanted was a cat with frickin' laser eyes. Was it so much to ask?

Anyway, the cat never, at any point, destroyed anything with its laser eyes, or even showed any signs of laser-eye having, so Bacon was sizzling with anger and wrote a strongly worded letter to Aristotle called the Bail Organa. I'm being told that isn't true either. It was called The *Novum Organum*, and it apparently wasn't actually addressed to Aristotle since he'd been dead for 2,000 years. But no doubt about it, Bacon was NOT impressed by Aristotle's deductive reasoning. In his frustration, he came up with a wild idea. He said, "We philosophers are trying to figure out how reality really is. How about we just LOOK at it? Instead of coming up with premises that appeal to our current biases and then trying to prove them deductively, we could just LOOK at the world and describe what we're seeing, even if that's not what we thought or hoped the world was like at the beginning. Listen, I really wanted a cat with effing laser eyes. But when I LOOK at my cat, it never looks like a cat with effing laser eyes. Maybe I should just take the measurement of *not even once seeing laser eyes* as evidence that maybe my cat doesn't have laser eyes. At the very least, maybe I shouldn't assume my cat has laser eyes since I've never seen him with laser eyes, even though I'd really love that. I have literally zero empirical examples of my cat having or using laser eyes. So maybe let's just LOOK at reality. In other words, maybe the first step of science is OBSERVATION, not INTUITION. What do you guys think?" (At least I'm pretty sure he said something like that.) Anyway, based on this insight, Sir Francis Bacon was given the appellation of "Father of the Scientific Method" due to the fact that looking at reality is sort of important if you want to understand how reality actually works. (And also due to the fact that he was from Europe rather than the Middle East.)

Around that exact same time, only a vigorous swim across

How to Think 67

the English Channel away, was a French philosopher named Rene Descartes.  He heard Bacon's plea to measure reality empirically in order to understand reality, and thought about it.  He thought about a lot of things, by the way.  He was sort of famous for thinking.  Anyway, he thought about Bacon's plea, and then responded, "Nah." And Bacon asked, "What?" so Descartes responded, "I think I'll just stick with the belief that rationality originates in the mind," and then he did that thing where he points both index fingers toward England and clicked his tongue.

Bacon thought that finger-pointing stuff was a little condescending, so he responded, "You know, that's a little condescending.  And condescending means 'speaking down to', by the way."  Then Bacon gave that little smiling slow-nod.  Not the "I found a kindred spirit" kind.  Or the creepy across the bar kind.  More like the "yo clapback, bro" kind.  He then continued, "What's up, man?  Why do you have a problem with, you know, just LOOKING?" Descartes, unable to come up with an acceptable clapback-to-the-clapback responded, "It's just...you know...how can we even trust our senses to tell us the truth about anything?  You feel me?  Maybe there's a demon playing tricks on my mind, or we're in the Matrix or something." (This is me "bending over backwards" to say that Descartes is making a really good philosophical point.  I may address it later.  But from a practical standpoint, it's totally irrelevant.) "Well," responded, Bacon, "um, are you asking whether you can trust literally the only thing that's kept your ancestors alive since the beginning of life on the planet. Tell me, what's your alternative?" And with that, Descartes pretended like he couldn't hear Bacon anymore and started his own mislabeled school of philosophy called Rationalism.

Wait! We forgot an important stop on our magic school bus in between Aristotle and Bacon (*I didn't really forget*). Let's jump back to the 14th century to visit a rather popular fellow named William of Ockham. Most people know him because of his infamous shaving accident known as Occam's razor. And to this day, no one knows why the "kh" turned into a "c". (*sometimes I'm just joking...they know...whoever they are*) Apparently it WASN'T a shaving accident, but a philosophical principle known as Occam's razor. Also, William wasn't the first person to come up with this idea. Even Aristotle had a very similar concept, but you know, you can't give Aristotle credit for everything, and William of Ockham didn't come up with deductive logic. So he got credit for this. Nice job, Billy, you get a gold star. Everybody knows what Occam's razor is, and almost everybody's wrong. Wait...what? Yeah, that's right, you heard me. Now pay attention. When I ask most people what Occam's razor is, I get a response such as, "Duh, it

How to Think 69

means the simplest answer is usually the right one." (*straw man*)

Now, William actually did vocalize a principle, and the actual principle is sort of like that, I guess if we're really stretching. But it's actually nothing like that at all. If you think that's what Occam's razor is, then listen with both ears, as if you have a choice. That's NOT what Occam's razor is. In our little visit here to the 14th century, I'm not going to explain what Occam's razor actually is, because I'm going to save that for our trip into the future! The future! Echo...echo! What I'm going to do instead is to explain why the popular misunderstanding of the razor is more or less useless if your goal is truth.

But it turns out that the popular misunderstanding is a really, really useful one (*if your goal is to create a straw man fallacy*) for many religious people, who love to define the principle incorrectly and then immediately shoot it down as weak sauce. Because in their words, it's "just a heuristic, and it doesn't always work very well." At least some folks say that. Other folks who don't know what heuristic means say it's "just a rule of thumb, and it doesn't always work very well". And why do they do this? Because when you're asking how David Copperfield walked through the Great Wall of China, if you really want to believe in magic, it kind of sucks to realize that David

Copperfield probably doesn't actually have magic. The "simplest answer" is that it's an easily explainable illusion, not a cool answer like Copperfield is in league with Satan. If you really want to believe in God, it kind of sucks if the "simplest answer" is that it just happened to coincidentally stop raining at the beginning of your speech, not that God made it stop raining. So it makes life so much more mysterious and gives plenty more room for miraculous intervention by God (*God of the gaps fallacy*) if Occam's razor is merely a heuristic, and not a very good one at that.

I mean, let's think about it. There are so many things in life where the "simplest answer" is certainly NOT the right answer. So maybe it isn't a very good heuristic after all. Bohr came up with a "simple" model for the atom. That thing was super simple. It's just a nucleus and little electrons orbiting around it like a solar system. That's what I call simple. And then later physicists said it was "too simple". How can that ever be the case if "the simplest answer is the right one"? And then you've got Newtonian physics (i.e., classical mechanics). The math for Newtonian physics is so elegantly simple it almost makes you believe in God. And of course I'm talking about the Christian God specifically, amirite? And then Einstein came along and demonstrated that the math was a little "too simple". What? Too simple? That makes

Occam sound utterly ridiculous. His heuristic couldn't possibly be right. Who are we going to believe here? Some yahoo from the 14th century who didn't even come up with his namesake principle, or the greatest mind of the 20th century, possibly of all time (*appeal to authority*)? Who are we going to believe, huh?

And another thing, what does "simplest" mean anyway? I mean, if simplest just means fewer words to describe how something works, then it's much, much simpler to just say that Copperfield used "magic" to walk through the Great Wall. Magic...that's one word. That, my friend, is very simple. If you have to go into all the mechanics of his sleight-of-hand and the apparatus that makes the trick work, that's way more complex. And why did the rain stop right when my speech began? Isn't the simplest answer "God"? It's only three letters for heaven's sake! That's even fewer letters than "magic"! Don't you dare start in with meteorology and weather patterns and such! That is complicated and befuddles the brain. It would be so much simpler if I just didn't think about that stuff at all, really, because I have no idea how meteorology works. Obviously Occam's razor isn't a very useful principle so I'll only use it when it works for my religious belief and toss it out as unreliable when it can be used against my religious belief. I mean William of Ockham was a religious guy anyway, right? It wasn't like he was trying to shave God out of the picture.

Okay, have I sufficiently described the problems with Occam's razor, at least as popularly misunderstood? Have I captured the essence of why we can't use the (incorrectly understood version of the) razor to question supernatural assertions and the like? If not, then feel free to write a letter. Give me the true straw man version of Occam's razor and we'll go from there. As I hear these arguments nearly on the daily, I'm going to move forward with the assumption that I'm probably pretty close. Occam did not ever say "the simplest answer is usually the right one." What he did say is, "plurality is not to be posited without necessity," and as it turns out that, my friend, is a very useful heuristic. I don't mean useful in the "straw man a principle so you can keep believing in a superstition" sort of useful. I mean the "actually grasp reality" sort of useful. William was NOT saying "the simplest answer is best." He was saying something INCREDIBLY PROFOUND. Something that if properly understood, changes the world. But in order to really understand what William of Ockham was actually meaning, we need to jump a bit more into the future.

Time to hop back onto the magic school bus and head to the late 17th century just in time to see...d'oh, we just missed it. Back up the school bus like 30 seconds. Okay look out the windows on the left side of the bus. See that apple tree over there? No! No! Your other left! For the love of...we just missed it again. Back up the school bus again. Okay, everybody, left side! See the apple tree, and the guy sitting underneath it? That's Isaac Newton. He figured out gravity from apples falling toward the earth, but more importantly realized that the earth was falling toward the apple as well. But even more important than that, he realized that the force that caused the apple to fall to the earth was the same exact force that kept planets in their orbits around the sun. That's the part that concerns us on our trip through the history of the foundation of science. Newton was one of the smartest people to ever walk the face of the earth (*apple to authority fallacy*). And he wrote a lot of very important things about the laws of physics. He figured out several laws of motion as well as other awesome stuff that still proves useful for measuring our everyday world experience. The rules start to break down as soon as things get too small, too big, or too fast. (Simplest answer isn't always the best, see what I mean? Anyway, that's not my point right now, but keep this in mind.)

He wrote down many of his ideas in his seminal work, the *Philosophiæ Naturalis Principia Mathematica*, but apparently, a bunch of people didn't like all the big words, so he just shortened it to the *Principia*. Within this work, he gave many answers to questions of physics that had baffled humanity since the beginning of time. But most important to our understanding of the foundation of science, he gave a set of rules that enabled him to come up with the answers that had baffled humanity. There are two rules in particular that interest us right now:

> Rule 1: We are to admit no more causes of natural things than such as are both true and sufficient to explain their appearances.
>
> Rule 2: Therefore, to the same natural effects we must, as far as possible, assign the same causes.

The first rule is critically important to understanding proper thinking, but we're going to come back to that one as soon as we hear from another very smart fellow on the topic (*appeal to authority*). In the meantime, let's discuss a few terms that are necessary for catching Newton's drift. First, Newton is talking simply about cause-and-effect. When any effect is visible and measurable, we call that a "phenomenon". A phenomenon is anything that expresses itself in the objective, measurable world. Its mere existence implies that something brought it into existence. And so whatever it was that caused the phenomenon, we'll call a "causal entity". A phenomenon might be the causal entity for another phenomenon (and often is), but when it plays that role of causing some other phenomenon, we'll call it a causal entity for simplicity when trying to explain the phenomenon that it caused.  The entire universe is made up of a deterministic chain of causal entities and phenomena that become causal entities for other phenomenal events.  But none as phenomenal as this book.

Any phenomenon that is expressed and measurable, simply by virtue of it being there and being measurable, means we must explain how it got there.  Right now, I can see the intelligent religious people rubbing their hands together and salivating out of both sides of their mouths.  On the one side of their mouth is dripping the words, *Cosmological Argument*.  The cosmological argument boils down to the fact that any phenomenon that is dependent upon another causal entity is known as a "contingent" phenomenon, therefore there must be some cause (the First Cause) that is contingent on no other causal entity.  *And of course that causal entity is God. Boom!  And I'm talking about the Christian god, of course!  Checkmate atheists!*

This is me "bending over backwards" to state that their point is very worthy of discussion.  And I may cover that later.  But for now, let me say that for our purposes, the origin of the universe is a scientific question and ultimately deserves a scientific answer, even if we don't have the tools necessary to answer it scientifically right now.  But what

Newton is talking about is an apple falling from the tree (i.e., the phenomenon) and the immediate cause of that apple falling from the tree (i.e., the causal entity). If he can answer that question, in the discussion about "what makes apples fall from trees in a direct line toward the center of mass of the earth?", as long as he can demonstrate a *sufficient* answer to that very specific question, we'll call it good enough. In other words, we don't need to explain the origin of the universe (or even the origin of the apple tree) to be satisfied with our answer of how the apple fell. If a glass falls off a table, but right before that, I saw the cat swiping at the glass with its devious little paw, I can call it a sufficient explanation to say that the cat did it. In other words, I don't need to go into the cat's genealogy to explain the immediate phenomenon under scrutiny.

The other side of the intelligent religious person's salivating mouth is dripping the words *quantum mechanics*. For those who haven't studied this, quantum mechanics is a branch of physics that studies the interaction of subatomic bodies. Turns out their interactions are very weird with respect to our normal everyday experience. Some people even call it a bit spooky. But the real cause of salivation is a specific set of quantum rules known as the "uncertainty principle" (and its oft confused cousin, the observer effect). The

## How to Think

uncertainty principle essentially states that, at a subatomic level, the deterministic chain of cause-and effect that I just described above breaks down into fields of probability. For example, we can figure out a particle's momentum OR is position, but we can never determine both with precision. Therefore, God. (*argument from ignorance...no, but seriously, people make this argument*) Ooh, those subatomic particles are more devious and wily than a cat's paw against a glass dangling on the precipice of the table. Who puts their glasses so close to the edge of the table when you have a cat in the house anyway? Schrodinger, that's who. But you can never guess when he will or won't.

I'm "bending over backwards" yet again to say that this is also a very good point, and worthy of its own book for discussion, but the abbreviated answer to this question is *computers*. Not quantum computers, which is another book by itself, but just regular ol' computers, like the kind you may be reading this book on right now. Computer programmers write deterministic programs. The computer programs follow a set of deterministic rules. And never, at any point whatsoever, does a programmer have to account for quantum uncertainty. There's never been a time in the history of computer programming when a programmer had to write special logic to account for quantum uncertainty. Deterministic programs run precisely the same every time. If God is using quantum mechanics to jump into the middle of a computer program and change something, he's really not doing a great job of making his presence known. When we're talking about macroscopic events, it's okay to describe the chain of cause-and-effect as deterministic. Stop with the "quantum mechanics, therefore God" argument. Please.

And now back to Newton's point with his second rule: "to the same natural effects we must, as far as possible, assign the same causes" (again, we'll discuss the first rule in a bit). Here's what he's saying: when one apple falls from the tree and then another apple falls from a tree, it's completely obvious to our everyday experience that whatever caused the first apple to fall from the tree ALSO caused the second apple to fall from the tree. But that's just an assumption that we make (no really, it's just an assumption), and there's no way to prove this with absolute certainty. It's possible that the first apple fell because of some force that we call gravity, but that the second apple simply moved toward the ground because it was being pushed by a little invisible demon...the kind with those little bat-like wings, can you picture it? And the demon also just happens to push apples toward the earth at $9.8 m/s^2$, which also just happens to be the speed of gravity near the earth's surface. Amazing coincidence, don't you think! Satan is tricksy!

Newton's point was, even if we can't tell the difference between the two phenomena, if there is nothing whatsoever that DISTINGUISHES the two events, then we should treat the two events as having the same cause. Now of course, both of the events could have been caused by gravity. And it's also possible that both of the events could have been caused by little demons with bat-like wings. But what Newton is suggesting is that logic and reason require us not to draw a distinction when we can't DISTINGUISH anything MEASURABLE between the two. And yes, it's important that any claims of distinction be objectively measurable. If we can't objectively measure any distinction, and yet we claim there's a difference between the two events, then we're basically saying that there can be no explanation for anything, because we have nothing to go on explanation-wise when the next apple falls to the ground. This doesn't mean we can prove with absolute certainty that the cause of Apple 1 falling is the same cause as Apple 2 falling. It simply means we can't distinguish between the two, so we must treat them as identical. This principle is foundational and critical to our logical understanding of how reality works. And if you aren't following this principle, you are not following logic. Religious thinking contradicts this principle all the time.

> Apple #1: Hey, it's raining today. It must be random metrological happenings.

> Apple #2: Hey, it's raining today, and while there is no OBJECTIVELY MEASURABLE way to DISTINGUISH this rainstorm from any other rainstorm, I wanted to go golfing today. So it must be God punishing me.

This type of faith-based thinking simply cannot take place at the same time in the same mind as rational, scientific thinking. And consequently, we can take this principle even one step further, just as Newton did, and try to roll-up even more events under the same cause. Newton did precisely this, and even though it certainly could have appeared to have separate causes, Newton used rule #2 to determine that the apple falls to the ground and planets revolve around the sun because of the same causal entity: gravity. Dude was a genius (*appeal to authority*). But, he really was. If you wish to think rationally, do not look for separate causes within indistinguishable phenomena. Look to assign the same causes to indistinguishable phenomena. You can't do both at the same time.

And now for our last trip on the magic school bus, we'll jump relatively close to the modern era: the mid-1900s, and peek in on a wild-haired chap named Albert Einstein. In physics books, Einstein's special relativity is often used to contrast against Newton's classic mechanics. Because ultimately, Newton was merely pretty close, and Einstein is presumably a bit closer. Newton wasn't really wrong per se, because his math works fantastic in our normal everyday experience, but starts to fall apart when we get moving really fast or exist near very large gravitational bodies. Anyway, this might be another really swell lesson in how the simplest answer isn't always the best or correct one. But that's not the point right now. We're only stopping in to visit Einstein for two reasons. First he's one of the smartest individuals to ever walk the face of the earth (*appeal to relativity*), and second, he gave a quote that parallels Newton's *Principia* rules in such an illustrative way that it merits a mention.

His definition of what we're talking about here covers all the salient points and helps us understand what William of Ockham was trying to say 600 years prior. And I bet we would have had hover boards by now if people had listened to William sooner. Or if people stopped thinking he meant "the simplest answer is usually best". Anyway, here's what Einstein had to say on the subject:

> "It can scarcely be denied that the supreme goal of all theory is to make the irreducible basic elements as simple and as few as possible WITHOUT HAVING TO SURRENDER THE ADEQUATE REPRESENTATION OF A SINGLE DATUM OF EXPERIENCE." ~ Einstein

No one is arguing that Einstein accidentally left his caps lock on halfway through his quote. And I'm not trying to yell through text. But the second half of the sentence is the portion I'm looking to call special attention to in this portion of the discussion.

But right before we get to that, let's look at the first half of the sentence. When he's talking about the "irreducible basic elements", he's echoing Newton's first rule to "admit no more causes" than what is SUFFICIENT to explain the phenomena. The goal of scientific thinking is to come up with a smaller and smaller list of causal entities that can explain all phenomena. (This is what they mean by "simpler".) But we can only reduce the list to "as few as possible". If some other theory can explain the same phenomenon with fewer causal entities, then whatever superfluous causal entity your theory has is simply UNNECESSARY. It serves no purpose when an explanation with fewer causal entities is already SUFFICIENT. So the goal of theory is to do away with all UNNECESSARY causal entities. (This is also known as parsimony and means the shaving away of UNNECESSARY causal entities. Hence the "razor" in Occam's razor. Don't shave too close though!) So we need to look at the word *sufficient*. Sufficient means you've covered the explanation. As I mentioned earlier, I don't have to get into the cat's genealogy to sufficiently describe how the glass fell of the table. The explanation to the question "How did the glass fall off the table?" can be

SUFFICIENTLY described as "the cat knocked it off with its devious little paw." So sufficient means "enough". But it also means "no more than is NECESSARY". Once I've described the causal effect that can sufficiently explain the phenomenon, I have no need to go any further. Of course, it's entirely POSSIBLE that an alien sent a message directly to the cat's brain, causing the cat to engage in an otherwise totally normal cat behavior. But "normal cat behavior" all by itself is SUFFICIENT to explain the phenomenon. So invoking aliens as an explanation is completely UNNECESSARY (and thus irrational).

So what about competing explanations? What about gravity vs. little demons with bat-like wings? Either of those explanations could be considered SUFFICIENT on face value, right? For right now, I'll "bend over backwards" to say that it's somewhat arbitrary which causal entity you use to explain the phenomenon, as long as you're consistent. If you want to insert "gravity", then great. If you want to insert "little demons with bat-like wings", then great. Just stick with your explanation when the phenomena are indistinguishable. However, if you do decide to insert "little demons with bat-like wings", you need to explain why they *always* behave like mindless automatons, *always* pushing apples to the ground at 9.8 m/s$^2$, and *never* deviating from this reality with their little devilish wills to disrupt the natural state of floating apples.

Why don't they ever act on their own will? The logical, reasonable answer is that it is an UNNECESSARY assumption to grant free will to the force pushing apples to the ground. It *never once* acts as though it has free will. A force lacking any sort of will is a SUFFICIENT explanation, and thus explaining it as a force that does have a will is completely and utterly UNNECESSARY. And by the way, even if you were to choose "little demons with bat-like wings", assuming that the demons have bat-like wings is *also* an UNNECESSARY assumption. Why do you keep saying they have bat-like wings? How does that assist the explanation in any way, shape, or form? Do they wear monocles and top hats as well?

So, that more or less covers what's meant by UNNECESSARY and SUFFICIENCY. But what do I mean by NECESSARY? Well the fact of the matter is, apples falling to the earth is a MEASURABLE phenomenon. And so if we're going to be reasonable, then we have to agree that a measurable event demands an explanation. Remember, rationality begins with MEASUREMENT. Which means there's a little open question...a little open space right there requiring an explanation for the cause of the event. Filling in that explanation is NECESSARY if we're going to explain what we are measuring. And just as a side note, philosophers do not appreciate or agree with my use of the word

NECESSARY here. The word NECESSARY is mostly used in relation to the Cosmological argument (described above). If you have a better word for what I'm talking about here, be my guest. But all I am acknowledging is that effects demand causes. I can use the causal entity of gravity over and over and over again without having someone come up with a better explanation (i.e., one that describes the same phenomena with the fewest causal entities). So we'll call it the entity that best fills the space of NECESSARY explanation, or the NECESSARY causal entity. So we can graph out the idea like this:

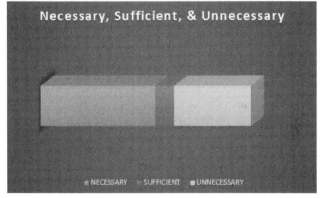

NECESSARY – gotta fill in this space, but be consistent
SUFFICIENT – enough, and no need to go farther
UNNECESSARY – no need to go here, seriously, you're stepping into the world of irrationality

Okay, now that we've covered the first half of Einstein's

quote as well as Newton's first rule, let's cover that second, all caps part: "WITHOUT HAVING TO SURRENDER THE ADEQUATE REPRESENTATION OF A SINGLE DATUM OF EXPERIENCE." For our purpose, "adequate representation" is the same thing as SUFFICIENCY. As long as you've filled in the blank for describing the cause, you've taken care of SUFFICIENCY. But wait! Have you really? Back in Newton's time, his classical mechanics explanation for bodies in motion would have been considered SUFFICIENT, but in the modern time, it's considered INSUFFICIENT. So what's the big diff? How can Newton's explanation be both SUFFICIENT and INSUFFICIENT? The answer always goes back to MEASUREMENT. Do you remember that measurement is the foundation of scientific thinking and rationality? It's no different here. At the time of Newton, they simply didn't have the tools to measure the difference in effect of super high speeds. And so it was *rational* in the 18th century to treat all bodies in motion as following classical mechanics rules. The classical mechanics rules were SUFFICIENT (at the time) to explain all measured phenomena. But today those rules are NO LONGER SUFFICIENT. We have more data than Newton had (and some of that data doesn't fit classical mechanics) and so we need to account for it. And so the rules need to be updated to explain the newly measured phenomena. In other words, we can only reduce the basic elements of explanation insofar as it doesn't "surrender...a single datum of experience."

If you propose a theory (such as classical mechanics), and someone raises questions that your theory doesn't account for, it's your job to demonstrate how your theory covers all measurements within the scope of the theory. If you can't do this, your theory is INSUFFICIENT. And it might just need to be updated with a more complete theory (such as special relativity). But either way, your theory must account for all data within its scope. And if new data comes along that your theory can't explain, then you need to update your theory. So the scientific explanation may or may not be updated all the time based on new measurements that cannot be accounted for under the current explanations of things. UPDATING SCIENTIFIC EXPLANATIONS IN LIGHT OF NEW MEASUREMENTS IS NOT A BUG IN THE SYSTEM. THIS IS THE SUPREME FEATURE OF SCIENCE. If you cling to an older explanation that no longer sufficiently explains all phenomena, then you are thinking irrationally. If you cling to an older explanation that assumes superfluous causal entities, then you are thinking irrationally. Zeus might have been a NECESSARY explanation for lightning in ancient Greece. But it is no longer NECESSARY now. And so believing in Zeus now is irrational.

So according to Einstein, we have to account for every "datum of experience". On the flip side, what *don't* we have to account for? If we've never measured it, we *don't need to account for it.* Hypothesizing non-measurable, phantasm-like entities and then asking someone to account for them is irrational (and yet, happens all the time in religious thinking). I don't need to account for leprechauns just because someone imagined them. I would only need to account for empirical measurements of leprechauns. To be rational, we need only account for what we can measure. But that doesn't mean that measured things are therefore the only things that exist. It's okay to hypothesize phantasm-like entities if no other MEASURED causal entity can account for a particular measured phenomenon. For example, we theorize the existence of dark matter and dark energy even though we can't directly measure these. But the most important part here is that we would drop them as a valid theory the very same second we could account for them with other measured causal entities. Because dark matter would become UNNECESSARY the very second we could account for its proposed effect in other ways. And the second most important part here is that we don't automatically assume that dark matter has bat-like wings and free will.

Okay, now that we've wrapped up our journey through

time to get a handle on the history of scientific thinking, let's recap the highlights. Rational thinking starts with MEASUREMENT of reality. It does not start with hypotheses or intuition or a priori ideas about reality. We don't go about rationality by coming up with explanations for things we haven't measured. That doesn't mean unmeasured things don't exist. It's just unreasonable to claim they do before they're measured (or as a last resort, they are necessary to explain something that has been measured.) It's okay (reasonable) to drop Zeus as an explanation for lightning when a measured explanation comes along. It's not okay (unreasonable) to keep clinging to Zeus as an explanation when a measured explanation comes along. Don't hypothesize more than is necessary to explain something.

Reasonable thinking is actually pretty simple. In fact, in many ways, this entire chapter can be summed up with a simple set of equations (*No! Math is not simple! How is this simplifying anything!*):

$A+B=C$

$A=C$

$B=?$

Can you solve for B? (*NO! I can't solve for B! This is not simple!*) If you paid attention in Mr. Thompson's pre-algebra class, you probably already know the answer to this problem. And the answer of course is ZERO. (*Those are all letters! You can't tell me the answer to a problem with only letters is a number!)* For those who didn't pay attention in class, why is it zero? With the substitution method, I can take the second equation (A=C) and replace either the "A" or the "C" in the first equation with the other letter, (e.g., replace the "C" with an "A", such as A+B=A). And then combine like terms and solve (B=A-A; B=0).

Of course, Mr. Thompson probably would have kept the attention of the kids in class if he told the story of Dumbo and written it out like this:

> FloppyEars+Feather=Flight
> FloppyEars=Flight
> Feather=?

Now recall that, at the beginning of the story, Dumbo was given a "magic feather" by Timothy Q. Mouse and was told it was necessary to achieve flight. Of course, Dumbo was terrified of jumping from the high platform (who wouldn't be?), but with the belief that only a magic feather could bring, he took a leap of faith and began flying around the room. This event is represented by the first equation. He has floppy ears and a feather with the resulting effect of "flight". Of course, later in the story, he accidentally drops the feather but yet is still able to fly. So no more feather, but he can still fly. What was the difference? Well, he still had those floppy ears. This second event is represented by the second equation. Using the substitution method, we can see that the feather was not ever necessary for flight in the first equation. (Though I will "bend over backwards" to say that it might have been necessary for Dumbo's courage.) We can describe both phenomena with one causal entity (i.e., the floppy ears), and can shave away the feather as being UNNECESSARY. *But I was told at the beginning of the story that the feather was magic and now you're trying to ruin magic for me!* Okay, yes you can cling to your original belief and toss out reason and rationality to continue believing. Yes, you can do that. But you can't be rational at the same time. And this is why the two methods of thinking cannot coexist in the same mind at the same time.

We can use this formula for all sorts of things. The cat knocking the glass off the table with the devious paw and aliens sending telepathic message to the cat to knock off the glass. Sure I can see how the cat could have done that without a telepathic message from aliens, but *you can't prove* that aliens didn't send a telepathic message! (*burden shifting*). Yes, you're right, I can't prove aliens didn't send a telepathic message to the cat. But as soon as you acknowledge that you can see how a cat could knock a glass off a table without the telepathic message, you've just written the formula of the second equation. And just like that, you've made the alien explanation irrational, because it's UNNECESSARY. The cat's paw is a SUFFICIENT explanation for the event. Any superfluous explanation is UNNECESSARY. And that, dear reader, is how to think rationally. In the next chapter, we're going to look at other characteristics of scientific thinking and how they support reasonable thinking. And don't be surprised if I "bend over backwards" to show some of the limitations of science. But spoiler alert: there isn't one limitation of scientific thinking that doesn't also apply to faith-based thinking (*tu quoque fallacy*).

This was another rather large chapter, so let's recap the highlights:
- Rationality starts with MEASUREMENT.
- The real difference between superstition and science is STATISTICS.
    - Statistics depend on measurement.
- MEASUREMENT is an inductive process.
- The first step of science is OBSERVATION, not INTUITION.
- Occam's razor ISN'T "the simplest answer is usually the right one."
- Don't surrender the adequate representation of a single datum of experience.
    - i.e, make your explanation SUFFICIENT.

- Limit your explanation to only that which is NECESSARY.
- Assign INDISTINGUISHABLE effects to the same cause.
- We don't have to account for claims that haven't been measured.
- A+B=C; A=C; B=0

# Chapter 4 – Why Science Works

Okay, folks, we made it through the most difficult material. And it wasn't even that difficult, right? Scientific, rational thinking is not that hard to grasp. Start with a measurement/observation. Come up with the best possible explanation. And by "best" we mean that it's the one that SUFFICIENTLY describes the observation without assuming UNNECESSARY causes. Stay consistent in assigning causes for effects, and try to limit that number of causes down to the bare minimum. That's all there is to it, right? Well of course that's not it, but these are critical first steps. And yes, it would be awesome if that's all there was to it. But unfortunately there's a bit more to it. In Chapter 1, I defined *rational explanation* as "any explanation for an empirical measurement that follows the established rules of logic". At the time, my critics were telling me that I can't get away with simply saying that the rules of logic are "pretty well established". In order to carry the burden of my claim, I have to actually explain what the rules are and why they are pretty well established. It's like at the fast food dive where they have that sign saying if we don't give you a receipt, you can have a free cookie. That kid at the cash register *always* gives me the receipt. But really, just one time I'd like to get that free cookie. Well, you're not getting the free cookie here either. But you're going to get

How to Think 95

something even better. We're going to talk about the rules of rationality. (...) No, seriously, it's much better. (...) Okay, fine, it's not as great as a free cookie. In any case, I told you I'd support my earlier claim, and here we are. In this chapter, we're going to go over some more of the rules of science and why we continue to use these rules.

It turns out, the rules of rationality are quite specific, and scientific/rational claims are actually highly constrained by these rules, which means that you can't just pull a theory out of your arse and call it science. Some of my more religiously-minded associates sometimes accuse science of doing precisely this. *Global Warming? Why, scientists are just making that up to sell lightbulbs!* The rules of science actually create very tightly defined bounds around what can and cannot be claimed. And the rules tie scientific claims to reality. Ironically, faith-based thinking doesn't have such constraints. Yes, the same constraints that religiously-minded people love telling scientifically-minded people they need to have around their claims. But think about this. Religiously-minded people often already know the rules of rationality and also understand their importance in making claims about reality.

But often the same people who complain about science making up "theories" have no problem walking into the church and buying wholesale claims that have no rational basis whatsoever (*double standard*). You can literally make up any claim you want and start a religion around that claim, even if it contradicts our measurements of reality. And in some cases, it's *because* it contradicts our measurements of reality that it draws such a crowd. Of course, religious thinking could choose to tie their religious claims to objective measurement. But if they embraced such a philosophy fully and completely, then they'd basically be science at that point, wouldn't they? And then what would be the point of religious faith? To whatever degree they diverge from this standard, they contradict scientific, rational thinking.

As we've done in the last chapters, we need to start by defining a few terms to make sure we're on the same page. What exactly is "science"? Science is happening all the time, and we talk about how "science says this" or "stand back! I'm going to use science!" So from the ubiquity of it all, it would seem that everybody is on the same page and we're all talking about the same thing. But like many frequently used words (*God*), people can have entire conversations around a topic and be talking about very different things. So let's be clear about what's being discussed here. Very frequently, when people think of science, they think of it as a collection of answers. Maybe at some point in the past, people thought the earth was flat. We've actually known it is round (*oblate spheroid...got it*) for much longer than is generally given credit, but at some point in the past people thought so. We claim to know the chemical composition of distant stars, and how far away Alpha Centauri is. And we know these things because of science. But this scientific "collection of knowledge" is not really what I'm talking about here.

Science is a philosophy. It's a way of thinking. It's an awesome way of thinking that aligns very well with rationality. But this way of thinking also has some drawbacks. And so it's important to "bend over backwards" and acknowledge them, so you know what you're working with. We talked about some of the underpinnings of scientific thinking in the last chapter. But the underpinnings go even deeper. Science is ultimately based on certain philosophical assumptions, which themselves cannot be proven (*gasp!* Did I just say faith? *gasp!*). When I use the word philosophy, this is where half the people fall asleep, and the other half get really mad, because "science is NOT a philosophy! It's the sure bedrock upon which we can build all truth!" Did I capture that sentiment correctly, Science Bros?

The unfortunate reality is that we might be living in the Matrix, and just as Descartes feared, it's possible that our senses are 100% wrong about everything we think they sense. If you want to demonstrate your senses are accurately sensing reality, how would you go about doing that? Via your senses? See the problem (*circular reasoning*). Descartes felt himself going mad even thinking about this, so for those uneasy with the feeling, I won't dwell on the possibility for too long. But we have to acknowledge that ultimately, everything we think we know about reality could be a lie, and we might just be Neo inside the Matrix. So the first philosophical assumption that we're making is that reality actually exists outside of our minds. No, really. I understand this feels counterintuitive, but this is just an assumption. We call this assumption empiricism. (Some people take empiricism to a much stricter degree than I do, but I'll get to that in a moment.)

Religious-thinking people are rubbing their hands together at this assumption, because "HA! You just admitted that we all use FAITH!" amirite? No. I've already defined faith as relying on UNNECESSARY assumptions to explain observations. We can say that it's "faith" to believe in gravity vs. invisible demons with bat-like wings, but we need to fill in the explanation of falling apples with something (so it's not the "faith" that I'm talking about). If you're going to live your entire life as though you are actually in the Matrix, be my guest. Make sure to be consistent though. But no matter how you choose to answer it, you're getting signals to your brain that make it appear as though there's a big world out there. And that measurement demands an explanation. In the film The Matrix, Neo traveled back into the Matrix after he had been popped out by Morpheus and his team (*not pooped out, but I can see that too*). He saw a noodle restaurant and remembered that he liked the food. But then pondered if his whole life was a lie. The reality is that regardless of whether the noodle shop was simply computer code, Neo could still take scientific measurements to judge the distance from his apartment to the noodle joint, for example. It's rational for Neo to say, "It's two blocks to the noodle joint," if repeated experimentation confirms that claim (and he has no better explanation for the existence of the noodle shop and his apartment). It's still a scientific endeavor from inside the Matrix to measure and explain things inside the Matrix, even if the entirety of the experience is a mirage. Our goal is to come up with the best explanation possible with the available information. Science isn't a set of stationary answers. They are all tentative. We might find out the world isn't round (*yes, oblate spheroid, got it. Can I just use *round* from here on out?*), but whatever measurement we take in the future to overturn our knowledge would need to better explain all the prior measurements. That said, our collection of measurements is being updated all the time, so we need to able to change with the times and update our theories to account for new data.

The second reason this doesn't help religious-based thinkers' argument *at all*, is because we're trying to make as few assumptions as possible (remember Einstein's quote from the last chapter?). Some religious people hear that we might be living in the Matrix, and take that as a carte blanche to believe whatever they want, and think we're all engaging in the same faith-based thought process. No. Whatever is making us believe there is a universe outside of our own minds is giving us measurements that demand explanations. But there is no measurement that demands leprechauns be assumed as the best possible explanation. Each proposed causal entity has to justify its own rationality.

The second term we need to define is "works" (I agree, it seems like overkill, but we still need to). In order to understand why science "works" we have to be on the same page regarding what is meant by it working. What I mean is that we can consistently rely on it. When we have to put it to the test, we can trust it. And the same set of explanatory assumptions can be used over and over again and they keep being repeatable and reliable. It's possible that you're just in a dream and like Vanilla Sky or Inception, you just need to leap off a building to wake up.

(As an aside, for those with suicidal tendencies, please, please do not do this. And for everyone else, ALSO please do not do this.) Most of us rely on the rules of gravity to work a certain way. And the rules consistently, invariably work this way. And so we take the elevator, not the 12th story window. An airplane flies according to consistent rules of physics that work. We can rely on those rules. To contrast, religious people often tell me that praying provides this same sort of consistent knowledge about the world. So I ask them to pray about the contents of a room and check their accuracy level versus my simply walking in to the room and looking. See the problem? No. Prayer does not "work" in this regard any more than my intuitive hunches work. So when I'm saying that science "works" I'm saying the methodology for measuring reality is more reliable than other methods. Science doesn't just work. It works much better than any other proposed method. I do NOT mean that science is right 100% of the time. I mean it helps us get to the reliable answer faster and more completely and consistently than any other method. The scientific method might get things wrong a thousand times, but it allows for correction and narrowing of the band of possible answers relatively quickly.

Alright, let's get that problem with empiricism (*straw man*) out of the way. If you slept through your intro to philosophy class, empiricism is basically saying that knowledge comes through our senses. Some scientifically-minded people diverge from my definition and state that the senses are the ONLY way to get knowledge. This is the hard definition of empiricism. Often this hard stance is referred to as "scientism" and religious people love to (*straw man*) this one to death. In their defense, many people who are more scientifically-minded argue from this stance. So I can't totally blame the religious folks. But that's not my argument. I have a much softer definition. As already explained, I acknowledge we could be in the Matrix, and so it's possible that our senses could be 100% deceiving us. And believing we're in the Matrix is the philosophical position of hard skepticism. I acknowledge that possibility, but am starting with the assumption that our senses are at least somewhat reliably conveying true facts about the universe. That doesn't automatically mean senses are the ONLY way to get knowledge. I'm certainly open to other methods of obtaining knowledge. But if someone has any suggestions for other ways to get knowledge, it's your job to demonstrate it, not mine.

And as long as we're talking about the problems of science, allow me to "bend over backwards" to talk about faith-based thinking in science. I love watching religiously-minded people criticize scientists who use faith-based thinking in their scientific works. First, because such work deserves to be criticized. When scientists do this, they're not doing science. They're doing BAD SCIENCE, which isn't science. There are many, many examples of this, but there are a number of famous examples of this really bad science. In the late 80s, physicists at the University of Utah claimed to have discovered Cold Fusion. This made world headlines because if it were true, it would mean the end of any sort of energy crisis anywhere. Of course anyone can see where they fell short. They were in such a rush to take the credit for one of the greatest discoveries of all time, they forgot to go back and check their facts. Turns out, the "Cold Fusion" effect was nothing like they purported it to be. In a more recent story, scientists from NASA thought they had discovered "arsenic-based lifeforms" and rushed the story to the news to get credit for their find, rather than rushing to check and recheck the data. And they brought embarrassment upon themselves as a result.

Yes, these are examples of faith-based thinking in science. And not examples of scientific thinking. The claim of Cold Fusion energy was a supernatural claim (without empirical support). I'm going to get to that in just a moment. But the point here is that, even if most people don't understand the underlying science behind the claims, most religious people can see the problems with the thinking that led to the mistake. These are not famous blunders because "science" made a mistake. These are blunders because these scientists were NOT DOING SCIENCE. In this chapter, we're going to discuss the rules they should have been following, and the rules that would have kept them from embarrassment. But the very human failings that caused them to blunder are very frequently celebrated within a religious context. We all know this is BAD SCIENCE, but it turns out their thinking is actually GOOD RELIGION. We'll talk about good science in this chapter, but also see how not following good science leads us astray. But more importantly, that bad science is nearly indistinguishable from good religion. It's a reminder to us all that this type of thinking is irrational regardless of the setting, whether scientific or religious. The difference is that religion rarely has good rules to compel us to think rationally. The faith-based rules of religion actually prey on our natural inclination to irrational thinking (*I said *prey* not *pray*, but I see what you did there*).

The second "rule of logic" is DOUBT. And doubt is better than faith. Oh, you don't believe me? And now you know why doubt is better than faith (seriously, pause and think about this for a minute. Maybe go read Richard Feynman's *Cargo Cult Science* and then come back. You seriously haven't read that yet? It's time.) Religious people criticize doubt (*notice the irony?*), but engage in doubt all the time. It's so easy for everyone to understand the benefit of doubt. Everyone uses doubt *all the time* on every belief out there *except* one's own beliefs. If you normally watch Fox News, think about how easily doubt comes to your mind when you hear that a story is being shared on CNN (or vice versa if you're a CNN fan). How easily "fake news" rolls off the tongues of people who feel no need whatsoever to support the assertion of fake news. Do you know what that's called when you doubt the credibility of CNN? That's called DOUBT. It's easy for you to do this. Let that feeling swirl around in the forefront of your mind so you can savor that sweet taste of doubt, and remember how familiar that feeling of doubt actually is to you. Now apply that feeling to Fox News. Or if you're a CNN junkie, apply that feeling to CNN. If you're like many people, you may notice how unfamiliar the two tastes are together in your mind because they may have never occurred in your mind concurrently. Scientific thinking demands doubt for sure. Everyone has the ability to doubt, yet most people do not use the kind of doubt I'm talking about. The doubt I'm talking about demands questioning one's own cherished beliefs. The Cold Fusion scientists would have saved themselves a lot of embarrassment if they'd spent more time in this mode of thinking. Faith-based thinking and doubt-based thinking cannot exist in the same mind at the same time.

I know some religious-based thinking people will say, "*But*

*I have questioned my religious beliefs! I question them all the time!"* This reminds me of a famous Noam Chomsky quote:

> "The smart way to keep people passive and obedient is to strictly limit the spectrum of acceptable opinion, but allow very lively debate within that spectrum – even encourage the more critical and dissident views. That gives people the sense that there's free thinking going on, while all the time the presuppositions of the system are being reinforced by the limits put on the range of the debate." ~ Noam Chomsky

There is a structure of rules surrounding the Santa Claus myth (*How dare you! He's not a myth! He's real!* Okay fine, I'll call it a "claim".) Someone who debates within the acceptable spectrum of the Santa Claus *claim* might argue strongly for how Santa might get down the chimney vs. having a magical key that opens any door. But this isn't really free thinking going on here, because the overall Santa claim structure is still firmly intact even after the debate is finished. The only way to truly engage in doubt about one's religious beliefs is to doubt the structure itself. The first debate presupposes Santa exists, and is only trying to make the claim make sense within the claim structure (*begging the question*). The second debate questions whether the Santa claim is supportable via empirical evidence, and then constructs the claim as supported by the evidence as the best possible explanation for the jingle bells you heard as you opened the shutters and threw up the sash.

If you haven't done this second form of doubt-based thinking, you haven't engaged in the doubt-based thinking I'm describing. In order for scientists to do science-based thinking, they must engage in this same type of doubt-based thinking with respect to their own scientific claims. Everyone who wishes to claim they are thinking rationally must engage in this type of thinking. DOUBT of one's own claims is the hallmark of scientific thinking. And while on the topic, I feel the need to mention again that I am NOT talking about self-doubt! Believe in yourself! Do awesome things with your life! But you are not your religious beliefs any more than scientists are their scientific claims. It's not only okay, but critical to criticize one's underlying assumptions. This is perhaps the most difficult principle to adopt, especially if you've reinforced faith-based thinking for the bulk of your life. This is easy to understand, but really hard to do. Our brains are wired to NOT do this (damn right I just split that infinitive...come at me bro). And so I understand why people often do not engage in this form of thinking. But the fact is that this form of thinking simply cannot exist in a mind at the same time as faith-based thinking.

Okay, well we talked about what is perhaps the hardest principle of rational logic...doubt. Now let's turn to what is perhaps the scariest part of science, unless of course you work in archeology, and you end up running into a lot of snakes. I hate snakes! (Speaking of which, can we pretend like *Kingdom of the Crystal Skull* just didn't happen? Not if we're gonna use science, Mister! Gotta count all the hits AND misses to do science.) Barring the "fear of snakes" kind of fear, the scariest part of science is making a claim. This may seem weird from a religious perspective where wild claims are made all the time with little to no regard of the claim's connection to reality. In science, you actually have to defend the claim with empirical evidence. And that's where the scariness comes in. In order to make a claim in science, you actually have to stretch your neck out in order to make that claim. You have to assert the world works a certain way and then demonstrate that it actually does. But religion makes claims all the time, and it's not that scary. So what's the big deal? The difference is that, within the realm of scientific thinking, you actually have to support the claim with evidence. And the claim has to be the most reasonable explanation for the phenomena. That actually takes a lot of work. And you end up with damaged credibility when you make the claim before you've really put in the time to doubt your own claims, as the Cold Fusion guys.

If you make a claim, you take on a philosophical position known as the BURDEN OF PROOF. It means you actually have to support your claim with evidence. The evidence must be empirical. It has to be accessible to everyone else for review and scrutiny. In other words, it must be measurable. If it's not measurable, then it's not evidence. A scientist cannot state that a claim is true simply because he is a scientist (*appeal to authority*), though in fairness, this sort of thing happens all the time within science. (And when it happens, that makes it BAD SCIENCE.) Appeal to authority is not a feature of science. It's a bug in human nature that science is, at least in theory, designed to weed out, and one that religion is often designed to prey on. ("Follow the prophet...don't go astray." You feel me, Mormons?) Burden of proof requires the claimant to support the claim. And as famously described by Christopher Hitchens:

> "What can be asserted without evidence can be dismissed without evidence."

If you refuse to accept the burden for your claim, then I am under zero obligation to accept your claim as valid.

If you say, "Dragons are real," I would respond, "Cool! I would really love to see them. Can you show them to me?" If you respond with, "Well, I don't have evidence that they're real. I'm just claiming they're real," I'm going to be really let down. But more importantly, I will simply dismiss your claim due to lack of evidence. I am under no obligation to now search the world over to prove dragons DON'T exist just because you claimed it. I'm just going dismiss your claim, but with a very heavy heart. See how simple this is, and yet how scary it is having to make a claim using the rules of logic?

This philosophy of BURDEN OF PROOF works exactly the same in a criminal court case. The prosecution is the claimant, and thus holds the burden of proof. The defendant is NOT making the claim, and thus holds no burden. The prosecution is claiming that the defendant broke the law. And so therefore, the prosecution must support their claim with EVIDENCE. People still have biases against the defendant and think he's guilty just because he has that guilty look on his face, or he bleached his hair as he was trying to make an escape to Mexico....you know, hypothetically speaking (*I'm looking at you, Scott Peterson*). But philosophically, the burden rests on the prosecution. If at the beginning of the court case, the judge asked the prosecution for evidence, and the prosecution were to say he had none, that would be the end of the case. The defendant wouldn't need to prove he didn't commit the crime. And in all likelihood, the prosecution should be disbarred for wasting everyone's time.  Just like you did to me when you claimed there were dragons.  Why did you get my hopes up?  Why?!  Once you've made the claim, then OWN YOUR WORDS.  If you make a claim that dragons exist, then you better demonstrate that they exist.  If you can't demonstrate evidence for your claim, then at the very least demonstrate some INTEGRITY/HUMILITY by withdrawing the claim, and apologizing for getting my hopes up.  Don't turn it around on the other person to disprove the claim.  And notice how a person's inability to withdraw a claim lacking evidence demonstrates EGO and HUBRIS.  Why did you even claim it in the first place if you didn't have EVIDENCE??!!

There is not one standard of burden of proof for scientific claims and another for religious claims.  The philosophical burden rests on the claimant regardless of the claim, because you're the one making the claim.  If you claim it, support it.  And sure, you can make whatever claims you want and not support it.  I can't stop you.  But such a claim is *not rational*.  You can claim that there were 3-5 million illegal voters in a presidential election.  But if you don't support that claim, then it's an *irrational* claim.  Our purpose here is to talk about how to think rationally.  If you refuse to support your claims with evidence, then you are refusing to be rational. You can't have it both ways.

Part of making a claim is limiting the SCOPE of the claim. The claim "There are no black swans" is quite a different claim than "there are no black swans in my room." Scope is a critical part of thinking rationally, and necessary to consider with the words we use when we're describing reality. Claims are simply words that either accurately describe reality or they don't. When they accurately describe reality, we say they are true. When they don't, we say they're false. "All cats have four legs" is a claim about reality. But there is a scope element to this claim, just as there is with any claim. In order to bear the burden of proof for this claim (and in order to verify the truth value of the claim), you'd literally need to observe every cat in the world (or is it the universe?) and demonstrate that each had four legs. And such a claim could be easily proven false by just one example contradicting the claim. But either way, the burden for such a claim still rests with the claimant. And of course, we can shrink the scope of a claim down to something like "all black swans are black" and feel like we're pretty clever. Because by definition, every black swan is black. But that actually says absolutely nothing about reality. If there were no black swans at all in the entire universe, it would still be true that all black swans are black. We call this kind of claim a "tautology".

Sure, it's a true statement, but it doesn't say anything about reality. And therefore it's an irrational statement.

The next principle of logic is FALSIFIABILITY. Some people get caught up on the terminology here. Don't blame me. I didn't come up with the word. But what it's definitely NOT saying is a claim needs to be false. *Hey listen up, Mister! The only way to be rational is to make false claims!* Um, that makes no sense. What it means is that the claim has to be testable in such a way that we can determine whether it's false. Your claim has to be able to PREDICT something in the objective world and then the outcome of the claim needs to be testable in the objective world. If you make a claim and then keep shifting the claim, then your claim is not really falsifiable, and thus not rational. Zeus used to live on Mt. Olympus until we could climb to the top of Mt. Olympus. So the claim shifted, and then he lived on the clouds. That is, until we could get to the other side of the clouds. Then, he moved to Mars or something. But a claim can always be adjusted in such a way to avoid any sort of scrutiny. Intellectual integrity demands that we frame the claim in such a way that it can actually be tested in some fashion. If you can't do that, then it's an irrational claim.

Also, people make claims which they also believe to be testable, but then make every possible outcome of the test a TRUE condition for the test. For example, I can flip a coin and predict that it's going to land on heads. Of course, if it lands on heads, then I can use that as evidence that my claim was true. But if it lands on tails, I can state that in some countries, that side is called heads. Not only does this show a lack of intellectual integrity, but there is no way this test is falsifiable. Every possible outcome supports the claim. And so the claim is useless. *Did you know I have magic powers? I can guess the color of the next car to drive by. It's gonna be blue! Oh, it was red? I meant within the next three cars. Still no blue car? I meant within the next 10 cars. The ninth car was blue? Yes! Nailed it! See my magic powers?* And now, this is me "bending over backwards" to say that science also adjusts claims when the evidence doesn't support a particular claim. I'm not saying the very act of adjustment is wrong. It's actually important. The distinction is when you behave as though your original assertion was true, even though the evidence didn't back it up. And second, once your claim reaches a level indistinguishable from random chance, the rational explanation for your "magic powers" is random chance. Remember the math equations from last chapter? (*Egad! Not math again!*) It works here too.

$$\text{MagicPowers} + \text{RandomChance} = \text{Effect}$$
$$\text{RandomChance} = \text{Effect}$$
$$\text{MagicPowers} = ?$$

Clinging to the original claim of "magic powers" at that point is irrational. And for that matter, asserting it as the most likely explanation from the beginning is probably irrational as well.

So your theory has to have a way of being disproven...at least in theory (why am I so poetic?). Your job as a claimant is to figure out a way to do that. Does that sound too difficult to do with your faith-based claims? It might be, but think about it: if you don't have a way to do this, why do you believe it in the first place? If you can't figure out a way to make the claim falsifiable, then why are you claiming it's true in the first place? Perhaps there's an invisible pink unicorn sitting behind you right now. You can't disprove such a claim. But if there's no way to prove or disprove such a claim, then why are you assuming it's true? Rational thinking, doubt-based thinking, and integrity demand that we look for *any* information that doesn't fit our own theories. We need to do everything in our power to make sure our theory accounts for all data. That is rational-based thinking. Faith-based thinking looks for a few examples that support the theory and then throws out contradictory evidence. You can't have it both ways. And you can't think both ways at the same time.

Okay, so up to this point, we have the following rules: (1) assume the world exists, (2) observe it, (3) make a claim about how the world works by (4) defining a scope for the claim, and (5) making the claim testable. Is there any part of this that seems irrational? Does everything so far seem reasonable? I hope you're okay with what we have so far, because I'm about to throw in another philosophical assumption. And that's the assumption of INDUCTION. Induction is making general conclusions from specific examples. If you saw the sun yesterday and the day before (and so on), you are using specific examples to conclude generally that it appears daily, and will continue to do so in the future. Based on those specific measurements, you're pretty safe claiming that it'll appear tomorrow. But there's no guarantee. This is what's known as the Problem of Induction. (And in case anyone cares, this problem was made famous by David Hume. Didn't think so. But I still like ya, Davey.) Either way, here I am "bending over backwards" again to show the limitations of science.

The famous example of the Problem of Induction involves black swans. The same friendly feathered friends we were discussing above in the section on scope. But let's discuss them a little differently here. Would you like to do that? If you don't, that's too bad. This is a book and by the time you read this, it'll be too late for your feedback. Let's say that for your whole life, you had only seen white swans. And so you felt pretty comfortable in your belief that there were no black swans.  If you think about what brought you to that conclusion, you'd see that it was induction.  You observed specific examples in reality and took measurements.  Every possible measurement (related to the question) came back with only white swans and never black swans.  And so (assuming you've actually put in a good deal of time to test this claim) it's reasonable to conclude generally that there are (probably) no black swans.  No guarantees, of course, but it would be entirely irrational to claim that there were black swans in light of the complete lack of evidence for black swans.  Then!  One day, you came across a black swan.  That one measurement alone would change everything.  It's no longer reasonable to conclude there are no black swans and completely reasonable to conclude there are.  Do you see how the claims are driven by MEASUREMENT?  If you wish to claim it, support it by measurement.

But in any case, this creates a bit of a philosophical problem for science.  If our sample of reality doesn't correctly represent reality, then our claim is actually wrong.  Yep.  Exactly.  I know what you're thinking.  This is a problem (they should probably call this the "problem of induction" or something).  So logic dictates that we take steps to ensure our sample approximates reality as closely as possible.  We can't be certain of anything, actually.  Maybe the sun won't come up tomorrow.  We can't know that it won't. But that's not how any of us live our lives. It's important to have humility about the limitations of our knowledge, but we have to move forward as though the past will predict the future. Because we have nothing else to go on. And so we make an assumption about future measurements based on current measurements. Isaac Newton described this in his fourth rule (Do you remember we already covered the first and second rules? The third rule actually pertains too, but we won't worry about that right now):

> Rule 4: In experimental philosophy we are to look upon propositions inferred by general induction from phenomena as accurately or very nearly true, notwithstanding any contrary hypothesis that may be imagined, till such time as other phenomena occur, by which they may either be made more accurate, or liable to exceptions.

In other words, we'll worry about the black swan when we measure it. Otherwise, we're going to live our lives as though there are no black swans until we see one. We live according to measurement, not imagination. *Oh no! But what if the black swan will punish us for eternity if we don't believe in it before having any evidence of it?* Well, that's kind of an abusive, petulant black swan, don't you think? Does that black swan want us to live our lives according to irrationality or something?

Lastly, on the topic of inductive logic, it's important to note that we are absolutely okay hypothesizing the existence of otherwise unmeasured entities if the inductive data supports it. As mentioned earlier, Pluto (too soon to bring up poor Pluto again?) was hypothesized based on measurements that weren't measurements of Pluto. Dark matter is hypothesized based on measurements that aren't measurements of dark matter. We can draw inductive logic from math, because math is simply an abstraction of inductive data. Our hypotheses still need to be the most likely explanation based on the available evidence and not hypothesizing UNNECESSARY entities. But what is not okay is hypothesizing the existence of black swans just because you really want there to be black swans and we haven't measured every inch of the universe (*swan of the gaps*).

Alright, we've laid down some rules of logic, how to make claims, and what we need to be willing to do with those claims. The claim itself needs to be falsifiable, which is a fancy way of saying that it needs to be testable. As it turns out, there are many strict parameters on how a claim needs to be tested as well. In this section, we'll look at how to conduct a scientific experiment, or least look at the process in general. There are many experimental methods in science, because there are many different kinds of questions. But most of the standard methods follow a similar pattern.

In order to do this, let's use an example of an experimental drug study. The drug in question is supposed to cure what we'll call DiseaseA. In this example, there's a drug manufacturer, and they've spent millions of dollars and plenty of hours developing the drug. They really want this drug to do well so they can recoup the manufacturing costs. I mean, who wouldn't, right? So they're going to do everything in their power to make sure this drug hits the market and also that they make a profit. Anyone see a problem with this example yet? *Of course those capitalist bastards want to kill us with their drugs in order to make a profit.* No, no, this is a totally upstanding drug manufacturer. They wouldn't hurt a flea. Even if we took them at face value as a respectable, conscientious drug producer, we still have to acknowledge that there is a bias involved here. They've spent money and need to make money. We're naïve if we think that won't have any impact on their practices. Similarly, individuals have biases as well. We don't want to die, for one, and so the thought that we might poof out of existence when our heart and brain stop is quite unnerving. We would be naïve here as well to think that personal bias has no impact on how people approach the question of death.

Does the drug really cure DiseaseA? Well, even though they've worked really hard on it, it turns out that the drug manufacturer is about the worst entity on the planet to answer that question for us. We need to test the drug in a way that completely removes the drug manufacturer's bias from the question. We need to perform a scientific experiment. First, we need an ethics committee. This is a body knowledgeable about the existing science on the question that is entirely removed from the profit channel of the drug, so their biases are not tainted by the profit. They need to be like a judge in a court case, removed from the outcome of the experiment to determine whether experimenting on people is justifiable. Of course, it's possible that dirty deals are happening in the background to bypass this impartiality. We have to acknowledge the possibility. But such deals are not a feature of science. They are a feature of human failings. The scientific process is designed to control for such human failings. Religion rarely has such controls over the same human failings. Both are true by design.

The ethics committee will want a plan for how we're going to test the drug. A very poorly designed experiment might be to simply give the drug to a few people and see what happens. On the surface it seems like a good idea, right? Weren't we talking about cause-and-effect earlier? Isn't this, like, *exactly* how to measure cause-and-effect? Give the drug, watch the effect.  Seems pretty straightforward.  Well, the problem is that it's NOT at all straightforward.

With such a poorly designed test, we have what are known as CONFOUNDING VARIABLES.  That's just a fancy way of saying that there are two or more possible causal entities for getting better.  Certainly if someone gets better, we know that the effect is "getting better".  No question there.  But what was the cause?  *C'mon, me.  Why am I making this so difficult?  We gave them a pill and they got better.  The cause of getting better is the pill, obviously...right?*  Well, it turns out that some people actually just recover from DiseaseA without ever taking the pill.  Like, by sheer random chance.  Or maybe all those people just happen to eat strawberries, or they all drive Hondas.  The problem here is that we have too many potential confounding variables to simply give people the drug and watch what happens.  Maybe some people would have been healed by the pill, but they eat strawberries and that somehow blocks the healing agent of the pill.  Let's call all of these other possibilities White Noise.  In other words, White Noise represents every other possibility for causing wellness sans the pill as well as every other possibility that might keep the pill from doing its job.  There are just way too many possibilities here.  When the strawberries actually healed the patient, but we attributed the healing to the drug, this is called a Type I error.  (Can you think of any ways in which faith-based "experimentation" leads to Type I errors? I can.) So because of all the potential confounding variables, we have to get creative in the way we approach the experiment in order to rule out any of the possibilities of the White Noise. So scientific experimentation is actually more than just LOOKING. It's looking in such a way that controls against White Noise.

One way that we do this is through CONTROL GROUPS. The goal here is to get a large enough number of participants for the study, and then randomly split the participants into two different groups. One group is referred to as the experiment group. They will be given the drug. The other group is known as the control group. They will be given a placebo pill. *Wait...why is this any different than just giving everyone the experimental drug?* This setup actually makes all the difference in the world, because it allows the study to filter out the White Noise. And the key is found in the fact that we can expect there to be a comparable amount of White Noise in both groups. Maybe you have a few people who eat strawberries in one of the groups. But if the groups are randomly divided with no concern whatsoever for who eats strawberries or not, statistically speaking you should have approximately the same number of strawberry eaters on both sides. If strawberries really do help cure

DiseaseA, then it'll help about the same number of people in both groups. In other words, we should see the same random effects from every other possible random variable expressed to about the same degree on both sides.

*Okay, but that doesn't really answer the question. If both groups are going to have the same White Noise, why did we even split them into two groups in the first place?* Because if the drug actually works, we're now going to see a different rate of healing in the experiment group vs. the control group. And most importantly, we can attribute the difference in healing to the experimental drug. Other possible causes of healing will be accounted for in the White Noise on both sides and cancel each other out. If there were 5 people healed in the control group due to random factors, we can assume that about 5 people were probably *also* healed in the experiment group due to random factors. But if another 50 people were healed in the experiment group, we can assume those people were healed due to the drug, and no other variable. In other words, we were able to set up an experiment that removed all confounding variables and left us with just the variable we wanted to study: the experimental drug.

Of course, it's entirely possible that not everyone in the experiment group was healed. In all likelihood those 50 people who were healed don't make up the rest of the entire experiment group. What are we really saying about the efficacy of the drug at that point? What we're saying is that there isn't a perfect one-to-one relationship between the drug and healing. It's a percentage. It's a CORRELATION. As with most causal relationships in reality, things aren't perfect. We can't say the drug will definitely heal you. There's a chance it won't. Life's a risk. And so we have to think in terms of percentage CONFIDENCE LEVELS. Remember a while back when said the only real difference between superstition and science is statistics? This is where the difference comes out. If we just gave the drug to some people and watched what happened, our bias will almost certainly tell us whatever we want to see regardless of how many people were healed. But either way, we wouldn't really know how many the drug healed, if any. And it's because we had no way to test the drug's efficacy statistically. With a control group, we can know what correlation there is between the drug and healing.

There are many different kinds of experimental methods. Using control groups is very popular, but not the only way experiments can be conducted. Ultimately, the goal in any scientific experiment is the same though...to separate out the confounding variables and isolate the specific variable under investigation. Even 400 years ago, Francis Bacon understood this concept of separating out confounding variables in a rudimentary fashion. His method was to list all the places where a phenomenon occurred, list all the places where it didn't occur, and then rank the occurrences according to degree. And from this, you should be able to determine which factors caused the phenomenon. Although his method was a little too simplistic, he grasped the idea of confounding variables. And that truth comes from measurement, not imagination.

The drug study test also needs to be set up with DOUBLE BLIND conditions. This means that the participants don't know which group they're in, and neither do the people administering the tests. Through this randomization process where no one knows which group anyone is in, it helps remove the bias of the participants as well as the administrators of the experiment. And this matters because of human bias. The goal of scientific experimentation is to control for White Noise and Human Bias. It's possible that people are just "healing themselves" due to their belief in the potency of the drug, even if they're just getting the placebo pill. By ensuring no one knows which group they're in, everyone has the same placebo effect, and so the placebo effect in both groups cancels each other out. Our buddy Aristotle believed that the only way to derive the truth of something was from one's own mind. The mind was the true compass that needed to be relied upon. Francis Bacon, the father of the

Scientific Method, said eff that noise. The only way to see the facts is by dispassionately removing the mind from the equation (as much as possible). These are two contradictory ways of approaching the question. You can't do both at the same time.

Our bias is to want things to be a certain way, and so that want (i.e., our bias) gets in the way of seeing things clearly. If you don't think you have a bias, you probably have a greater bias than most. You can't fix a problem you can't acknowledge. If you are unaware of your biases, they are almost certainly tainting your ability to see reality clearly. Mormonism, the religion I grew up in, placed a great amount of weight on receiving "thoughts and impressions" as a sign of divine revelation, i.e., that God was speaking directly to your thoughts and feelings. According to the Book of Mormon (Alma 32) if you don't receive these impressions, it's because you need to put more effort into really believing you will receive the impression. Now, of course, it's certainly possible that there is a God and he communicates with people in precisely this same way. You can't prove there isn't! (*burden shifting*) Unfortunately, such a claim has confounded variables. And one of those variables is a bias to want to believe that you're receiving messages from God, as well as regular ol' feelings you can talk yourself into having. Not only is the Mormon "experiment" not controlling for one's own biases, it's actually reinforcing your biases, which virtually ensures you will convince your mind that you received the "revelation". The Mormon "experiment" runs completely contrary to scientific experimentation. It turns out there are a number of ways to control for this effect in the Mormon "experiment". But spoiler alert! It doesn't work out too well for Mormonism's claims.

Let's wrap up this chapter with a few more heuristics for removing bias from your testing of claims. The first heuristic is PEER REVIEW. The key idea to remember here is that human brains are designed to reinforce our own preconceived beliefs. We want to believe what we already believe. It's a vicious cycle, but I'll bet it was super helpful in the past. My town's football team is the best football team on the planet! And if you don't like it, you can get out! When a contrary opinion comes along questioning the certainties of our beliefs, most people's initial reaction is to attempt to expunge the contrary opinion. It's a tough thing to realize maybe your hometown's team can't even win the bottom feeder bracket. And it's especially tough to see this if you only talk to devoted fans from your own hometown. They're all going to back up your opinion that your hometown team is the best. And if you don't back them up, you're a fair weather fan, right? But with everybody in town backing each other up, it gives everyone the impression that perhaps your hometown team is actually the best. I mean, that many people can't be wrong, can they?

Peer review is designed to control against this personal bias for one's own beliefs. We looked at this principle tangentially when we discussed the role of the ethics committee. Their job is to ensure the experiment doesn't cause unnecessary pain, distress, or danger to the test subjects. So the ethics board is more focused on the humanity of the experimentation, but the underlying principle is still that of a group of dispassionate people controlling for the human bias of the experimenters. In other words, this is a form of REVIEW of the experimentation process. The drug company has every incentive in the world to do whatever is necessary to get that drug to market, so they might cut corners on the safety of the test subjects in order to boost their profits.

Peer review is more commonly understood to be a process that occurs after the experiment, allowing other people knowledgeable in that particular field to review the experiment and help point out flaws in the experimental method or results. You know who I'm talking about here. He's the teacher's pet who corrects other kids' answers and then gets made fun of at recess, Mr. Know-it-all (*ask me how I know*). The nail that sticks up gets hammered down. For some reason, in Japan that social conformity somehow makes all the kids smarter. Yet in the United States the conformity makes kids anti-intellectual. What's up with that? This needs to change. Anyway, in science, that Mr. Know-it-all is a hero. Pointing out mistakes is a benefit and blessing to the experimenter. It's the process the Cold Fusion folks should have gone through before they went public with their results. The Cold Fusion folks were certainly intelligent people. They didn't lack the technical knowledge to understand why the effect wasn't what they thought it was. So what was the problem? The problem is that they didn't really want to see the issues with their experimental method. This is bias. We all have biases. We all have things we really want to believe are true. And so we go out of our way to gather information that supports our beliefs, and we also go out of our way to discount information that contradicts our beliefs. We need people who disagree with us to check our work. We need people who disagree with us to point out the errors in our reasoning. Don't push away contradictory opinions. Seek out contradictory opinions, and let them help you see the problems with your beliefs.

If our goal is truth, then contrary opinions are not only doing us a favor, but providing a critical service that we cannot do ourselves. We can't see our own blind spots. We need someone who sees from a different perspective to do this for us. This is why I like to do what I call the

THREE POINT TEST. For ideas I want to believe are true, I will run them by three different groups of people. First, I go to the PROPONENTS of the idea. These are the folks who have bought into the idea completely. They are the evangelists trying to talk you into the idea. They have all the talking points for why that idea is the greatest idea since Google Glass (*too soon? RIP Google Glass*). And they can't see anything wrong with the idea at all. The idea is perfect and holy and sacred. And their input on the question is important, because they'll tell you everything good about that idea.

When I was a missionary for the Mormon church, and people would tell me they had heard something negative about the Mormons, I would ask, "Well, would you go to a Chevy dealer to learn about Fords?" The implication was that they should instead talk to us missionaries to get the "real truth". The unspoken point was that the Chevy dealer has a hidden bias and agenda against Fords and would only tell me the made-up bad stuff. Therefore, I should obviously only talk to proponents of an idea, never the detractors. Nah. That's crazy. Of course I should talk with the DETRACTORS. If the first group to talk with about Fords are the Ford dealers (the PROPONENTS), then the next group I should go to are the ones who dislike Fords the most (presumably the Chevy proponents). Sure, talk with the Mormon missionaries and understand the best arguments for their beliefs. And then talk with people who vehemently disagree with Mormonism. Yes the detractors have an agenda. (*so do the proponents*). Everyone has a bias. The problem isn't so much the bias, but the inability to recognize that everyone has a bias. Once you see that everyone has a bias, you can use that to your advantage to get different viewpoints and compare them to one another. Make bias work in your favor, not against you.

The third group are the NEUTRALS. Wait, I just said everyone has a bias, so how can anyone be neutral? It's impossible to completely escape your own bias. But the fact is people are more passionate about certain things than other things. Do I wear boxers or briefs? Depends, actually (*boom! Get it?*). (No, actually I have a very strong opinion about this question and am not dispassionate. I'm not neutral on underwear choices.) But there are many other topics for which I may have extensive knowledge but am quite removed from emotionally. I'm not neutral when it comes to underwear choices. But I'm NEUTRAL in other subjects, or at the very least, I'm more neutral. The goal is to seek out knowledgeable neutrals and get their opinion on the subject as well. A judge will never be perfectly neutral, but there may come a time when a particular judge has a conflict of interest with the case in question. Perhaps a judge is related to one of the parties in question. Or the judge may have stock options in a company being sued. In these cases, those judges should recuse themselves from those cases to avoid partiality. But in most everyday cases, the judge doesn't know the parties, and isn't personally vested in the outcome of the case. This is a NEUTRAL, even if there's no such thing as perfectly neutral. They're certainly more neutral than the PROPONENTS or DETRACTORS.

The goal of discussing with these three groups is the same goal of any scientific pursuit: finding the CONVERGENCE OF FACT. If you think about the three groups' opinions as being a Venn diagram, you might notice that the Ford dealer and Chevy dealers may disagree on quite a bit. Their opinions may not overlap on much. Mormon proponents and Mormon detractors may have very little harmony in their opinions regarding Mormonism. We expect this because they are ideologically opposed. They have competing biases that keep them from agreeing with one another. And yet...there are facts about Fords that both Ford dealers and Chevy dealers will likely still agree upon. There are incontrovertible facts about Mormonism that, as much as Mormon proponents love Mormonism and as much as Mormon detractors dislike Mormonism, both groups must agree are true. This is a CONVERGENCE OF FACT.

Looking at an issue from perspectives as diametrically opposed as one can, and still finding certain facts to be true, it's a good likelihood that that fact is true.

Mormon detractors have claimed for years that the meaning of the Egyptian text in Mormonism's Book of Abraham is nothing remotely close to Joseph Smith's translation. Professional Egyptologists who have no vested interest in Mormonism one way or the other concur with this assessment. And more recently, the Mormon church itself has stated that the text doesn't match Joseph Smith's translation, even though they have every reason in the world to wish it were otherwise. Where all these opinions converge is likely the truth of the matter.

Convergence of fact also means that the more you keep scrutinizing something, the more it keeps proving itself to be what it actually is. With just a quick glance, it might be easy to mistake vodka for water. But the more you investigate, the less vodka will appear to water, and the drunker you will become. Water, on the other hand, will continue to exhibit "waterness" no matter how many experiments you perform on it. No matter how many times you check it, water will keep on appearing to be water. Because it's water. The truth is that water is water. All the different ways you can possibly think to inspect water will lead back to the same point. That is convergence of fact. When magicians use a secret apparatus to make their illusion work, they usually only want you to inspect a certain part of their prop (i.e., the part that isn't the secret). If you could fully inspect it, you'd easily learn the secret. So they only show you the parts they want you to see. They're trying to fool you by keeping you from seeing the full picture.

So when you are testing the truth value of a claim, don't fool yourself. Don't conduct only those few experiments that keep you from seeing the difference between vodka and water. Keep digging until you find the convergence of fact. In other words, follow Richard Feynman's advice to "bend over backwards" to demonstrate how you might possibly be wrong. You still haven't read *Cargo Cult Science* yet, have you? In any case, you can't be fearlessly looking for any possible way in which you might be wrong and at the same time fearfully cowering from opportunities to see how you might be wrong. These two mental states cannot exist in the same brain at the same time.

Once again, let's do a brief highlight of the chapter:
- Science is a (tentative) collection of answers.
    - But more importantly, science is a way of thinking.
- Science is based on some assumptions that cannot be proven. (gasp!)

- Science is useful because it's reliable. (i.e., it works)
- Faith-based thinking *does* exist in science.
  - When this happens, it's bad science.
- DOUBT is better than faith.
  - DOUBT of one's own claims is the hallmark of scientific thinking.
- Making a CLAIM is scary because you have to support it.
  - This is called BURDEN OF PROOF.
  - Claims need to have SCOPE and FALSIFIABILITY
- The goal of scientific testing is to disentangle CONFOUNDING VARIABLES
  - Also, we have to figure out how to remove our personal bias from the equation
- Look for CONVERGENCE OF FACT.

# Chapter 5 – How Faith-based Thinking Works

For the last couple of chapters, we've explored some of the primary characteristics of reasoning and which elements are necessary to describe a thought process as rational. In other words, we've discussed HOW TO THINK. But there's an implication here that if you aren't using the methods and characteristics as described, then you aren't really thinking. Or at the very least, you are thinking incorrectly. And yes, to one degree or another, that is precisely the implication I wish to make. The whole point of this book is to discuss HOW TO THINK. So...yeah. That's what I'm going for here. Some ways of thinking are more valid and rational than others. And some are simply not rational because they don't follow the rules of rationality.

The words "thinking" and "thought" can have multiple connotations. So as in other chapters, it's necessary to define what is meant by the word in order to discuss the term. Certainly it's possible to think about the word think (*can we get any more meta?*) as simply meaning an idea arises in one's mind and then one is aware of that idea. Yes, that's one possible definition for thinking. I don't know where it came from, but right at this moment the idea of an ice cream cone popped up in my consciousness.

I became aware of that thought and then went and ate an ice cream cone. Because ice cream cones are delicious. Where did it come from, where did it go? Those are really great questions, Cotton Eye Joe. But that's not what I mean when I say "thinking".

Hey! An alien with eyes like Kermit the Frog just popped into my head and I became aware of that mental concept. Does that mean I'm currently thinking? Well sure, according to some definition of *thinking*. But that's not the definition I'm using here. There are a million different definitions for *thinking*. But we need to get focused and agree upon a definition if we're going to discuss the term rationally. So NO, that's not thinking in this particular discussion. Here, we're talking more along the lines of CRITICAL THINKING. In this discussion, "thinking" is using rational judgment. It's "using the mind to consider or reason about something." For this discussion, if you aren't using the principles and tools of reason, then you are not thinking.

It may not feel like it to some, but I've actually been pretty generous with faith-based thinking by referring to it as "thinking" up to this point. And I'll probably still refer to it as thinking in the future for simplicity. But it's not actually thinking in the sense we're talking about. Does this seem too harsh? Perhaps, but at the very least, it should be acknowledged that faith-based thinking is a starkly different form of thinking than rational thought. This isn't just an abstract argument here. No sir. There's a biological, cognitive difference between the mental processes I'm describing. But let's first talk about the similarities, how mental processes begin, and then where they diverge. While it may not be a perfect segregation of duties, the brain is subdivided into specialized areas that perform distinct functions. The first part of the brain under discussion is the prefrontal cortex. Without the prefrontal cortex, the kind of reasoning I'm describing in this book would not be possible. The second area is known as the limbic system, made up of several smaller areas, and comprises the source of emotion, including our fight-or-flight emotional responses.

There are some schools of thought (*see what I did there?*) that argue ALL mental processes first start as emotions, and not as rational thought. Sorry Science Bros, but even science doesn't start with a rational thought. It starts with measurement of the empirical world (i.e., the senses), and is followed by enough emotional wonderment and awe to motivate a person to investigate what it is they measured. The receptors in our eyeball light up when struck with light. Ideas work in a similar fashion. Ideas make us feel a certain way, and if we really like the idea, we start coming up with all kinds of reasons to support that idea. And if we don't like an idea, we come up with all kinds of reasons to expunge it from our brains (yes, I'm going for a record number of times using expunge in a book. It's a personal goal, don't rain on my dreams). This isn't true solely for faith-based thinking. This is true for everyone. The limbic system is powerful. It wakes us up in the morning and gives us a reason to live. We need emotions to move us. Why does someone like Nickelback? Who knows, but the point here is that the "reason" doesn't really matter. The person who is moved emotionally to like Nickelback may come up with "reasons", but ultimately they are just moved emotionally. That's it. We like things because we like them.

This is where the two modes of thought diverge. Without understanding the differentiation of various roles of the brain, Francis Bacon realized that the secret to understanding reality required that a person figure out how to dispassionately remove one's emotions from the equation. Even if the idea started in the limbic system, the only way to validate the truth of the idea would be to dissociate from the limbic system and examine the idea with the prefrontal cortex. In other words, the only way to see "reality as it really is" would be to figure out a way to Constrain Your Brain™ (yes, I'm trademarking that shit, and inside an already copyrighted work. Come at me bro.) In order to do science, you have to remove the passion from the testing results. If you can't do that, you're not doing science. It's nearly impossible to remove passion from faith-based thinking (or at the very least, I have yet to hear of a way in which this can be done). In fact, the emotional passion is a necessary ingredient in almost all faith-based systems. Tapping into your limbic system to strengthen belief is encouraged. Faith-based groups often advocate the avoidance of exposing your beliefs to the prefrontal cortex as thinking about your faith tends to minimize belief in it. Choosing to engage your prefrontal cortex and trying to avoid engaging it are simply incompatible methods of thinking. These types of thinking aren't even physically happening in the same part of the brain.

The fight-or-flight response is one of the most powerful and primitive emotions in human nature. When there is a sense of mortal danger, the amygdala goes berserker, wakes up its more primal neighbors, and they start sending chemicals into the system (such as adrenaline) to prepare the body for WWE SmackDown. Where the prefrontal cortex generally acts as the "executive function" of the person under normal circumstances, the amygdala's call to arms helps to shut down prefrontal cortex functioning. Instead of tapping in to a rational response when there is danger, the amygdala seeks out the help of even lower brainstem functionality to simply react without thinking.

The rational executive function and fight-or-flight response are two opposing controls over the brain. In a very physical, chemical sense, fear is the opposite of reason.

Many faith-based groups understand this all too well. But this is certainly not just a religion issue. Media organizations are often built on this premise. Fear sells much better than a human interest story. "If it bleeds, it leads." News outlets understand that higher reasoning function shuts down and takes a back seat when overwhelmed by the threat of danger. And so they pack as much fear-based news and fear-based advertisement into their programs as they can. I don't think news companies do this simply to get their jollies from people being afraid. It's because fear sells. They're in business to make money just like any other business. If you don't have Product X, you are going to *die this instant!* The Mexicans and Muslims are coming to kill you! Close up the borders NOW! Many exclamation marks!!! If human interest stories pushed products, the news would be filled with human interest stories.

And so FEAR is actually the foundation of faith-based thinking (in most cases). Fear leads to faith. Don't believe me? Within the Christian community, certainly there are plenty of people leaving these faith-based communities nowadays. And of course there are a smaller group of nonbelievers who join Christian communities. But almost exclusively, for nonbelievers who join Christian communities, the primary motivation is FEAR. Responses are almost invariably a concern for one's immortal soul. Or, being unable to come to grips with the possibility that one might simply cease to exist when one dies, one joins a religious community to reinforce the belief that one won't die when one dies. On the flip side, those leaving these same religious communities often do so precisely because they've lost that "fear of death", or rather, simply accepted that life will not continue after death. The two motivations cannot be more perfectly opposed to one another.

And this point can be further demonstrated by a little thought experiment. Consider a world in which people didn't die, or even where we collectively lost our fear of death. Assume we figured out the magical immortality pill and the result of everyone who took it. Churches would shutter their doors almost immediately, because no one would be seeking out solace for that dreaded "fear of death" and looking for improbable answers to that darkest of questions. Everyone would just live their life without any sort of concern about "what happens after death?" because fear of death would no longer be a concern. Essentially the same thing would happen if we took a pill that simply removed our fear of death. And this is all because FEAR IS THE FOUNDATION OF FAITH-

BASED THINKING.

And I get why people want to have faith in supernatural claims. This is not to say that I can't empathize with why someone wants to believe. Personally, I don't want to die. I like life. I like being alive, and if it were possible, I would live for thousands of years to see the future, which I have positive hopes for. Of course I would love to know that there is a happy afterlife waiting for me, where my deceased friends and relatives are there and at peace, and that there is an all-powerful being looking out for my well-being. In honesty, it is somewhat terrifying thinking of the possibility that these things aren't true. There is basis for fear to consider that my existence has an end. There is a basis for fear to consider that my life is not being protected and watched over by a guardian angel. But that basis for fear is the whole point. A belief in guardian angels comes from fear that no one is protecting you, not from evidence for guardian angels.

If you have measurable, logically supported answers to questions (and this is true even for fear-based questions), you do not need faith. It's solely because there are dark corners out there for which we don't have explanations that people seek faith-based answers. We don't know what's going to happen to us when we die. So we seek irrational answers to allay the fear, since no rational answers exist. We can talk ourselves into amazingly absurd ideas when we're afraid. But once you're holding an irrational belief to stem off a primal fear of death, you've set yourself up a nearly contradictory position against rationality. The fear of death creates a fight-or-flight response to any information that might demonstrate that your irrational belief is irrational, which shuts down prefrontal cortex processing of that information. Are you seeing the problem? This is how religions use fear to create a mental titanium wall of protection for their adherents' beliefs, even for the very intelligent adherents.

Once the titanium wall of belief protection is firmly in place, there are a number of irrational techniques that faith-based organizations use to reinforce the wall. The first technique is the IMMOVABLE MIND. A few years back, in a widely-publicized debate, famous Young Earth Creationist Ken Ham and "Science Guy" Bill Nye debated one another on the topic of science vs. faith. They covered many sub topics, but one of the most famous questions was essentially "What would change your mind?" Ken Ham responded that he takes the Bible as the inerrant word of God. He's totally convinced of that fact, and so no one will ever change his mind on that fact. In other words, his belief is unshakable. His mind is IMMOVABLE, and he takes this as a virtue.

Bill Nye on the other hand said, "Evidence." In other words, the scientific, rational position takes it as a virtue to change one's mind when presented with better evidence. Stephen Colbert famously quipped that President George W. Bush "believes the same thing Wednesday that he believed on Monday, no matter what happened Tuesday." When Bush heard this, he may have in fact laughed along because he may have truly believed such a "stay the course" stance to be virtuous. But is such a stance actually virtuous? Let's say you remembered the *Ghostbusters* apparition was called the Jet-Puffed Marshmallow Man, and you were insistent that was the case. And then you rewatch the movie and realize he was called the Stay Puft Marshmallow Man throughout. And not one time was he ever called the Jet-Puffed Marshmallow Man. Because Stay Puft is the term Ray keeps using, and it's written on the band of his cute little sailor's hat. And that's his name. How useful is the virtue of the IMMOVABLE MIND in light of all evidence contradicting your belief? How is this even considered a virtue at all? It may sound reasonable when you are protecting a belief based on fear. But in nearly any other setting, you would consider such a virtue to be absurd. If you struggle to think of an example (outside of protecting your religious belief) where the IMMOVABLE MIND is virtuous, *perhaps it's not a virtue*.

In debates with religious folks, I often hear a response such as, "But we change our minds all the time! The light is getting brighter and brighter every day!" Yes, there have certainly been updates to the Judeo-Christian faith since the Bronze Age. I grant that. But generally, like the Noam Chomsky quote from the last chapter, there are only certain issues about one's religious belief that can be questioned. The structure itself cannot be questioned. In other words, you have a SACRED COW. The IMMOVABLE MIND cannot ever question whether the SACRED COW is sacred. *Why do you have that stick here in your religious shrine? That is no stick! That is the Holy Staff of Starrin. Well, it looks like a stick to me. Stick!? Burn the heretic!* The purpose of a SACRED COW is to deflect criticism and legitimate questions by simply making them unquestionable. It's the last line of defense against any affront to belief. And the rationale to protect SACRED COWS is to reiterate that they are sacred (*begging the question*).

Sacred cows and an immovable mind simply cannot exist where rationality is involved. Rationality might be emotionally motivated (just as all ideas probably are), but it's the very act of intentionally devising methods to remove emotion from the equation that makes it rational. Rationality requires precisely a mind that is movable. It requires a mind that says, "I'll move with the facts, no matter where they go." It's like Hoban Washburne said:

"I'm a leaf on the wind; watch how I soar." (Still too soon? Probably...because it'll always be too soon.) Wash couldn't have landed *Serenity* if he were simply following a set of rote flight instructions. The situation required spontaneity and going with the flow of the actual physical conditions at that moment. The rational mind requires the same. The IMMOVABLE MIND clings to Bronze Age ideas regardless of the currently known facts. But conversely, the rational mind cannot cling to SACRED COWS. Rational thought must allow for *anything* to be questioned, even cherished beliefs. You can't cling to a SACRED COW and think about it rationally at the same time.

In the last chapter, we discussed the concept of Convergence of Fact, which is the more you keep scrutinizing an idea, the more the results keep supporting the theory. In other words, all of the facts converge on the same point. And wherever that point lies is likely the truth. No matter how many times I drive to where I believe my home is, it's still there. The more the results of observation continue supporting the theory, the stronger the case for the theory is. So what's the opposite of Convergence of Fact? And anyone want to bet the opposite of Convergence of Fact is a common attribute in faith-based thinking? We have a winner!

The opposite of Convergence of Fact is what I like to call the ONE-HIT WONDER. We can think of Convergence of Fact like The *Beatles* (Where were you when you realized the name was a pun? Be honest, was it right now?), Elvis Presley or Madonna. You may not like any of these performers (what's wrong with you?), but they were definitely reliably popular. They had a lot of hits, just like a good scientific theory has many more hits than misses. On the other hand, *Los Del Rio* had one, and only one song that made it to hit status in the United States. Can you name that song? If you guessed *Macarena*, you'd be right. (C'mon, you line danced to it in the 90s, admit it.) Unlike The *Beatles*, the music of *Los Del Rio* was not reliably popular, even though it was momentarily sensational. Similarly, faith-based thinking tries to find that sensational connection between their belief and reality. And let me "bend over backwards" to admit that such sensational connections do exist and do occur. There are weird things that happen in reality, if by weird you mean random chance. But if you want your claim to be taken seriously as truly being reasonable, it needs to do better than random chance. It needs to be repeatable, testable and the facts need to converge on your claim. In other words, you need evidence that isn't a ONE-HIT WONDER. Do you ever find yourself clinging to that weird random thing that seemingly supports your belief? You might have ONE-HIT WONDER thinking going on. This type of thinking simply isn't compatible with the rationality of CONVERGENCE OF FACT. And why are these incompatible? Because Convergence of Fact thinking looks at all possible data and tries to find anything that disagrees with the theory. ONE-HIT WONDER thinking keeps looking until it finds that one shred of evidence that seems to support the belief, and then throws out the rest of the contradictory evidence. You can't do both of these at the same time.

One of the most important aspects of scientific thinking is PEER REVIEW. This topic was discussed at length in the last chapter. We're all susceptible to "confirmation bias", which is the desire to believe information that supports what we already believe and throw out all contradictory evidence that doesn't support us. But Science Bros act like scientists are so smart. So why can't scientists review their own work then? Because confirmation bias isn't just how faith-based thinking works. It's how anyone's thinking works, and it's a huge problem for anyone trying to see things rationally. So we need someone else to review our work. Preferably someone who doesn't think like us. Remember the Cold Fusion guys? They were presumably well-trained scientific minds working on scientific research. Yet they couldn't see their own blind spot. Why? For one, that race to be the energy solution saviors, and the resultant fame and money that would follow, might have made it difficult to see the problem with their research. The failure wasn't the scientific method. The failure was not using the scientific method before rushing the research to the press. We're all susceptible to confirmation bias, which is why we all need some form of peer review.

When it comes to addressing our own biases, faith-based thinking works in nearly the opposite way of rational-based thinking. Rather than seeking out opposing voices to question our biases, faith-based thinking seeks out an ECHO CHAMBER of voices to tell us what we already believe, so we can believe what we already believed to begin with (*bandwagon fallacy*). People love validation. Birds of a feather flock together. We gravitate toward people who support and validate us, and we also steer clear of voices that disagree with us. This is me "bending over backwards" to acknowledge this bias is true for all of us. But the difference here is that science tries to create institutions that force us into the uncomfortable situation of having to listen to people who disagree with us even though none of us like that. And institutions based on faith-based thinking prey on our bias to flock together with like-minded people, telling us what we already believe to reinforce the belief. As a Mormon, I would attend a monthly "testimony meeting" where members of the church would stand before the audience and "testify" about the "truths" of Mormonism. This was literally preaching to the choir, because the choir was there too. And I know, because I was in the choir. The entire meeting is designed to ensure everyone hears exactly what they already believe to reinforce their beliefs, and nary a word contradicting their beliefs. The leader of the meeting is even instructed to cut off "testimonies" that contradict the teachings of Mormonism to ensure as near perfect ECHO CHAMBER as possible. Religious adherents, for the most part, aren't sitting in the pews to question their belief. They're looking for that sweet release of limbic system chemicals (which they call "feeling the spirit"), so the circular process of confirming your biases of believing your beliefs can be reinforced in the most potent way possible. These two methods of approaching biases cannot be more contradictory.

Let's conclude this chapter by discussing two techniques used extensively by faith-based thinking to reinforce belief: OBEDIENCE TO AUTHORITY and CONFORMITY. Now, this is me "bending over backwards" to acknowledge that these same techniques are used extensively in scientific circles. The point is that when science does this, it's running contrary to the principles of science. When faith-based thinking engages in obedience to authority (especially "revealed" religion), it is using one of the core pillars of faith-based thinking..."just gotta have faith!" And what exactly is faith being placed in? Some

AUTHORITY figure. Ask any Christian what the basis of their belief is, and you're likely to hear "The Word". The Bible itself becomes the source of authority for them, of course backed up by the authority of the interpretation of their local pastor. In fairness, many regular Christians are better at delving into the historical basis of the Christian claims than the religion I grew up in, but ultimately it all comes back to the circular reasoning of "The Bible is true because the Bible says the Bible is true" (*begging the question*).

I frequently get the impression that many people think they aren't susceptible to obedience to authority. If you don't think you're susceptible, you might actually be more susceptible than most. Okay, if your name is Sophie Scholl (who took on Hitler in Nazi Germany at age 21), you might not be susceptible. But in nearly every other case, you are probably just deceiving yourself. There have been a number of scientific experiments demonstrating that nearly all of us are susceptible to some degree. Before discussing these, it's important to note that all of the test subjects were tested for mental fitness before the testing began. These were all average, typical people. In other words, they were you and me.

The first experiment is known as the Milgram Authority Experiment. A test subject was brought into a room with another person (believed to also be a test subject, but was in fact a confederate) and told he was going to be randomly selected to be either the "teacher" or the "learner". But the selection was, in fact, not random. He was placed in the role of the teacher with the instruction to use a device administering increasing levels of electrical shocks to the learner (who is now in a nearby room) every time the learner missed a question. The teacher was even told that the highest level of shock could be potentially lethal to the learner. The learner intentionally missed questions to force the teacher to administer higher and higher levels of painful shock. Before you worry about the learner too much, it's important to note that the learner was never hooked up to the electrical shock. And even though the teacher heard increasingly louder screams from each shock, it was actually just a recording being played in the next room. The test subject was told the purpose of the experiment was to test the effect of pain on learning, but the test was really to see if he'd be willing to administer that lethal dose of electricity, just because.

It's the "just because" that's the whole key to our discussion here. Why would any mentally healthy, stable, typical individual administer a lethal shock to another person for getting a question wrong? "Just because." In this situation, the experimenter was sitting near the teacher, and when they started to falter and ask to stop, the experimenter would say something like "This is for science. We must continue." And then they'd continue! For science? What does that even mean? You're potentially killing someone, but you are willing to kill someone "for science"? The experimenter may have just as well said, "Just because" for all the faith this typical person put into the explanation. Turns out, nearly 7 in 10 test subjects went all the way to what they believed to be the lethal shock. And *every* test subject was willing to administer at least 300 volts. Just because.

The second experiment is known as the Asch Conformity Experiment. A group of people were brought into a room and sat in a line of chairs. All of them were confederates except for the very last person in the line, who was the test subject. They were shown one reference line and three comparison lines, as shown in the following image:

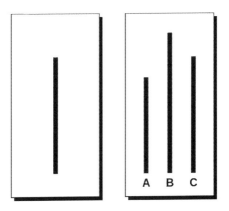

They were simply asked to decide which comparison line was the same length as the reference line. In this example, the correct answer would be A, of course. (Did I throw you off for a second there? The answer is C, not A.) The key to this experiment is that the test subject was told this was a "visual acuity" test. In other words, they thought this was just a test of their eyesight. But the point was actually far different. After the group was shown the lines, the experimenter would go down the row of people and ask them which comparison line was the correct answer. Each person would give the same incorrect answer. And then at last, it fell to the test subject to give his answer. It may seem counterintuitive, but nearly 40% of all test subjects gave the same wrong answer as the rest of the group, presumably to fit in with the rest of the group in most cases. But, some people said that the wrong answer everyone else gave actually did look like the correct answer. I guess we could argue that 40% of the population has really bad eyesight? Except they ran the same test on individuals (i.e., without a line of confederates ahead of them), and less than 1% got the answer wrong. So we can safely say the groupthink of CONFORMITY played a pretty major role in people getting the wrong answer. Even when we know we're choosing the wrong answer, peer pressure can make us do absurd things. But based on the self-reporting of people from this experiment, people's actual perception of reality can get skewed by groupthink as well. These people didn't think they were deceiving themselves. They really believed the wrong answer was the right one. Conformity to the group can actually make us believe absurd things. Faith-based thinking reinforces obedience to authority and conformity to the group.

When I was a child, the Mormons gave me a little resizable ring with a green shield and the letters CTR stamped on it...Choose The Right. The point was to have a tangible reminder with you wherever you went, to always do the right thing despite the peer pressure endured as a youth. And I still think the ring and reminder is a great idea. The irony was that the greatest peer pressure, the greatest attempts to force me into conformity and obedience to authority came from the Mormon church itself. What is the "right" anyway, if it's not that which mirrors reality as it really is? And what could be more wrong than believing something "just because"? What could be more wrong than "Just gotta have faith, man!" Voltaire famously stated, "Certainly anyone who has the power to make you believe absurdities has the power to make you commit injustices." The greatest dangers to the world today are those that compel people to commit atrocities upon others "just because". The danger comes in faith-based thinking. As demonstrated in this chapter, of course scientific institutions can use these same techniques. But it's precisely when they don't use the constraints of science that it can be allowed to happen. Faith-based thinking not only lacks these constraints, the opposites are virtues of faith-based thinking. It is critical to think for yourself. And this requires surrounding yourself with people who *don't* think like you. There can't be a more contradictory approach between faith-based thinking and rational-based thinking than in this regard.

We began this chapter by discussing the neurological processes occurring in the brain that cause these nearly contradictory ways of thinking. Rational-based thinking requires a good deal of effort from the prefrontal cortex. Faith-based thinking occurs mostly in the limbic system (i.e., the source of emotions) and is often driven by fear...fear of death, fear of outsiders, etc. I hypothesize this is the very reason civilizations with effective social safety nets end up becoming irreligious. The less people worry about where their next meal is coming from and also don't worry about catastrophic health problems because of access to a universal healthcare system, the less they rely on those fight-or-flight parts of their brain. When the amygdala isn't running full bore on a constantly heightened alert, the brain relaxes, and the pathways to the prefrontal cortex can be opened and used more freely. We need a world in which prefrontal cortex pathways are used more frequently. Fear is not evil per se. There is a benefit to having a fight-or-flight response in certain circumstances. There's even a benefit to having this response cut off prefrontal cortex processing of information for short stints of time when there is genuine danger. But this *cannot* be the standard mode of thinking for most people most of the time. It is dangerous for our world. Fear cannot be the constant ruler of the brain if the goal is to have rationality prevail.

# Chapter 6 – Case Studies

I hope you've been having an enjoyable time as we plumb the depths of rational-based thinking, as well as contrasting that to faith-based thinking. While there are several ways in which they are similar, there are so many ways in which they are not only dissimilar, but also contradictory. The same person cannot be doing both at the same time. I like to watch movies and get lost in the magic of improbable things. Science fiction and fantasy are the source of some of my favorite stories. I really like getting lost in a story, to suspend my disbelief for two hours, and really fall into the world created by other people's imaginations. It's fun. It's a great release from the constraints reality puts on what is probable. In some ways, it's like a drug to forget about commitments and responsibilities for a short while.

But it's pretend. I know I'm just enjoying the imaginative part of my brain for a bit. This make-believe may in fact be a necessary part of being a healthy human being, but when I'm engaged in such thinking, I'm not getting the neuron-firing wires crossed, nor blurring the lines between fantasy and reality. Okay, maybe a little bit with *Crouching Tiger, Hidden Dragon*. I really want to make my body light enough to float atop swaying bamboo forests like they do. And if they hurried up with that hover board from *Back to the Future 2*, that'd be great too. But even if the hover boards do become reality someday, it'll be because the inventor tapped into true principles of reality, not by dwelling solely in fantasy. We have to understand how things actually work in order to create things that don't currently exist. We have to be able to separate fantasy from reality. We have to be able to think rationally.

For this chapter, let's look at some CASE STUDIES of ideas people believe through faith-based thinking. We'll use the concepts we've discussed in the book up to this point to see the faulty foundations actually upholding the belief. And then perhaps most importantly, we'll then view the belief through rational-based thinking. Of course, if you don't already believe in one or more of these things, it will be obvious why that particular case shouldn't be believed anyway. But if you do believe in something on this list, pay attention to whether it raises your hackles to have it discussed in the same list of other ideas you consider to be false. Really dig into that feeling and see if you can find what is causing the emotion to arise. My hypothesis is that it's one or more of the attributes of faith-based thinking we've already discussed up to this point.

Before beginning the case studies, let me cover one point that is true for each of these. This is the same point I

made in chapter 1. Any one of these ideas could theoretically be true. Near the beginning of the book, I said:
> It's possible that you believe in something currently classified as supernatural, and yet that belief might be entirely true. Science hasn't disproved leprechauns, for example, and they would be classified as supernatural at this time. According to established rules of logic, it is irrational to believe in leprechauns.

It's important to note that at NO TIME am I saying any of these ideas are automatically false. I'm saying that it's irrational to believe in them. And I'm also saying that you cannot believe in them and think rationally at the same time. Alright, let's look at the individual cases.

### Extraterrestrials Visiting Earth

Do you know what I would love more than anything else in the universe? Benevolent aliens visiting earth and giving us their technology, hopefully with the know-how to live forever as well as their faster-than-light transportation technology to travel the universe. I would love this. My bias is hoping this were true. Whenever I hear a story about distant stars mimicking strange Dyson sphere-like behavior, I get my hopes up that there's someone out there waiting to make contact with us just as we are with them. And with a universe so vast, I don't think it's irrational to believe in the possibility of this being true. It's irrational to claim that it IS true, but certainly rational to accept the possibility.

However, that's not quite what I'm discussing here. I'm talking very specifically about an advanced alien species actually visiting earth. While it's been relegated to the occasional science fiction movie nowadays, since the 50s, belief in alien visitations still garners a cult following of sorts to this day. A popular question for astronauts is whether they see something "unexplained" out there. And man, I'd love to hear something that makes me believe they have. Even though there may be weird things at times, unfortunately there's always a rational explanation if you take the time to really look hard enough. Rationality ruins all the fun. Sorry 'bout that.

But what about crop circles? What about eye witness testimony of people who have been abducted by aliens? What about secret government documents revealing the truth of aliens? Let's look at these through the lens of reason. First, each one of these things is a MEASUREMENT of reality. If you've ever seen a picture of a crop circle, you've measured a crop circle. Do you remember earlier when we discussed how rationality begins with measurement? We're safely on the path of rationality when we accept the fact that there is something measured here and it needs to be explained. We remain on the path of rationality when we come up with an explanation for the measurement that follows the established rules of logic. So let's do that.

So we've measured a crop circle (i.e., we've seen a picture of one). Seriously that thing is exotic and strange. But all we can say at this point is there are crops and there's a weird circular design in the crops. I already mentioned my bias is to want to believe in aliens. So I start feeling all tingly and excited about the possibility when I see a picture with the description of "Possible Aliens?" (*very leading, poisoning the well...your honor, he's leading the witness!*). Using rationality, I recognize those tingly, excited feelings are actually my emotions feeding my bias. *I want* this to be true. But you know, "if wishes were fishes" and all that. My wanting this to be true doesn't make it any more true than wanting to win the lottery. Anyway, the goal here needs to be laying aside my biases, rather than allowing them to overtake my brain, cutting off the pathways to my prefrontal cortex, and look at this rationally. And with that, I've overcome the first hurdle to rational thinking: recognizing my biases are working against me and then looking for ways to constrain my desire for it to be true in order to let the facts speak for themselves.

Many crop circles are large, elaborate, and complex. And although someone might immediately proclaim such designs impossible!!! (many exclamation marks!!!) for humans to produce, the reality is there is no design that couldn't have been reproduced by humans. How could such a perfect circle be drawn in the crops like that? Did you ever take a geometry class? Perhaps amazingly for some, you can create a compass with a long rope staked to the center of the circle and you walking around the perimeter. This is not rocket science. So unfortunately, we have a CONFOUNDING VARIABLE. We have two (or more) possible explanations for how that perfect circle was created. How do we separate the variables out? Well, one way is create a SUFFICIENT explanation by removing any causal entity that's UNNECESSARY. Hmm, unnecessary....unnecessary. Which potential causal entity is unnecessary here? I could say ropes and stakes and compasses are unnecessary, but then I'd have a lot of other things I used to have sufficient explanations for that no longer have an explanation. How did I go rappelling the other day if ropes aren't real? How did I keep my tent from flying away if stakes aren't real? Pretty sure ropes and stakes are real. So what's left? Let's see...uh oh...that leaves aliens on the chopping block! NO!!! But I really wanted to believe in aliens! I'm going to weep and wail and gnash my teeth until I've convinced myself that aliens are the only possible explanation for crop circles, even though the crop circles can be easily explained by ropes and stakes and creative artists!

And do you see how that limbic system kicks right back in, trying to convince us to believe what we already want to believe, despite the fact that it's an unnecessary, irrational explanation? It's unfair because I so want aliens to be true and supported by the existence of crop circles. But if I lay aside my biases and desires and use rationality, I must conclude that crop circles cannot be used as evidence of aliens. Of course, I haven't ruled out the possibility that aliens did in fact create that crop circle. But clinging to that possibility isn't rational either (*burden shifting*). It's not the job of rationality to disprove aliens did in fact create them. Its job is to show which causal entity I can do without.

Eyewitness abductions and secret government documents can unfortunately be explained in a similar fashion. There are alternate explanations for these things that don't rule out aliens completely, but provide an explanation that makes alien visitations UNNECESSARY to explain anything we've ever measured. But do you know what would be awesome? Something that *can't* be explained in any other way than invoking alien visitations. Why do aliens always go to extremely remote areas and make themselves known to a small number of individuals?

How to Think    167

Why don't they plop down in Times Square, call a news conference with all the major news sources, with independent video being taken on many individual's phones cameras, and lots of time for anyone to come visit them as they wish? Certainly if they have the technology to travel light years away, they have the ability to do this. Oh, that's right! Government conspiracy! All of the governments in the world are working together to keep a perfectly concealed, watertight secret, even though they can't agree on trade policy. Got it. See the problem here? The alien explanation now requires even more unmeasured, unnecessary causal entities in order to keep everything afloat. Unfortunately, rationality requires us to accept ropes and stakes as the more likely explanation even though our biases would love for it to be the more exotic explanation.

A bit earlier, I mentioned a Dyson sphere, a hypothetical contraption surrounding a star, sucking its energy into the contraption to greatly increase the amount of energy a civilization can harness from the star. There have been several recent sightings of unexplained light output from several distant stars, and the sensational, leading headlines talk about possible Dyson spheres. Of course, my limbic system goes into overdrive thinking about the possibility, but the scientists measuring the phenomena are a bit more reserved. I guarantee most anyone being paid to study such things has the same emotional hopes I do. They want it to be a Dyson sphere or something cool like that. But despite their desires, they are carefully studying it, trying to disentangle confounding variables to remove any other possible explanation for it. In other words, they are trying to do science, rather than immediately jumping to their desired conclusion. You simply cannot be reserved in your judgment and jump to conclusions at the same time. These are contradictory modes of thought. In the meantime, it's simply not rational to conclude Dyson spheres surround distant stars or aliens as explanations for crop circles, even though we really want it to be true. Even if that's actually a Dyson sphere, and even if aliens really created that crop circle.

### Good Guys with Guns

Oh boy, now I've done it. It's all fun and games to critique someone's religion or belief in aliens. But don't ever go near someone's politics. *Second Amendment!* (*appeal to authority*). Can you feel the amygdala going into overdrive right now? Let me make a few statements to calm the limbic system before we get too far into this. First, I understand how hard it is to amend the US Constitution, and also how unlikely it is to happen any time soon. Don't worry, gun folks, your guns aren't going anywhere soon based on what I'm saying here. Second, the US Supreme Court has almost always sided with the second amendment interpretation that it's guaranteeing individual gun ownership, not simply a militia. Third, with political discussions, there are often two or more valid viewpoints, just as there are an infinite number of invalid viewpoints. The goal here is just to look at the question of "Good Guys with Guns" rationally, not to take away your guns. Are we okay now, or are you still worried about bad guys breaking into your house late at night?

Let's start by addressing something obvious...if there's any discussion that takes the amygdala to DEFCON 1, it's a discussion about guns. The discussion surrounding guns taps into the most primal of emotions, self-preservation and fear of being attacked by a predator. So if you hope to have a rational conversation about them, good luck. There's no quicker way to shut off the pathways to the prefrontal cortex than to bring up guns. It's probably safe to say that, for the most part, the driving motivation for guns is fear. When a perceived threat grows, gun sales rise. Even if the perceived threat is irrational. And perhaps especially when the perceived threat is irrational. The amygdala isn't concerned about some silly reasons anyway.

Now, allow me to "bend over backwards" at this point to say gun owners frequently raise a valid point. It usually sounds something like this: "If someone breaks into your house and starts doing bad things to your family, you're going to wish you had superior firepower!" And I will happily concede the point. We all have primal fight-or-flight responses to danger. There may be a few exceptions to this (I know some people who have made vows not to defend themselves from mortal danger, for example), but for the most part, most of us want to stay alive and would eagerly choose to kill someone bent on killing us rather than be killed by them. Personally, my amygdala generally kicks into fight mode, and I rarely feel the tug of flight mode when confronted with perceived danger. The complement to this argument is that I'd also wish I had superior firepower if someone came to blow up my house with an Apache helicopter. But I don't see too many people advocating the mass ownership of Apache helicopters, since the detriments of going that direction would easily outweigh the benefits. Do the detriments of general gun ownership outweigh the benefits as well?

Cue "Good Guy with a Gun" argument. *When you're in a public place, and Bad Guy pulls out a gun and starts firing, you're going to wish you had "superior firepower" to stop him. Think of how many lives are saved! We need more guns, not less guns! Let me tell you about the time Good Guy stopped bad guy with a gun! Therefore, don't take my guns away!* Have I captured the essence of the argument? There's one main problem with the argument...and that's STATISTICS. Do you remember in chapter 3 when I wrote: "So the only real difference between superstition and science is STATISTICS"? If the claim is not supported by statistics, it's simply not rational. At best, it's anecdotal. Usually gun advocates will point out a few stories where a Good Guy with a gun actually did stop a Bad Guy with a gun. Let's be honest here though, what you've argued at that point is that a Good Guy with a gun can at best *mitigate* the loss of life, not stop it completely. Because Good Guy only goes to work *after* people are being shot. But do such stories exist? Sure.

What it fails to account for (besides the fact that it's merely mitigating deaths rather than stopping them altogether) is that the anecdotal stories are not supported by the statistics. The FBI published a study of the 160 "active shooter incidents" in the United States between 2000 and 2013 (feel free to read the study yourself: https://www.fbi.gov/file-repository/active-shooter-study-2000-2013-1.pdf). What it found was less than 3% of the incidents were ended by Good Guys with guns. There were actually a higher number of incidents stopped by Good Guys *without* guns restraining the Bad Guy (about 13%), and far more (nearly 30%) were stopped by law enforcement personnel. In other words, it's superstitious thinking to believe that Good Guys with Guns is the solution to the problem. The narrative is simply not supported by the facts. What is the actual solution to the problem? I won't address that here (remember, scope is important, and such a question is outside of the scope of this discussion), but the key takeaway should be that the national discussion on the topic needs to be based on rationality, not superstitious, faith-based, fear-based thinking. We need to find ways to calm the amygdala before we can even discuss it, because the discussion will go nowhere rationally while limbic system pathways are governing the brain.

**Mormonism's *Book of Abraham***
In Chapter 4, I briefly touched on the subject of Mormonism's *Book of Abraham* in order to discuss the concept of CONVERGENCE OF FACT. Mormon detractors, Mormon Egyptologists, and non-Mormon Egyptologists all agree that the ancient papyrus the translation was supposed to derive from doesn't correspond to the text Joseph Smith produced. You'd think the issue would be case closed at that point. But evidently not. There are still people who believe in Joseph Smith's claim. So let's talk about CONVERGENCE OF FACT a bit more to see where the facts converge. For those who don't believe the claim in the first place, it may seem overkill to go to such great lengths to demonstrate

how the facts converge. But for someone so tied up emotionally with the claim, who has everything to lose (belief-wise) if the claim is actually untrue, it still won't be far enough. Either way, the point here is to demonstrate that it does not follow the principles of rationality to believe the *Book of Abraham* is what Joseph Smith claimed it to be.

Joseph Smith's work tells a story about an attempt on the Biblical Abraham's life when he was young at the hands of an "idolatrous priest of Elkenah," and then later tells of Abraham visiting Pharaoh in Egypt to reason upon the principles of astronomy. On the other hand, the ancient papyrus is actually a common Egyptian burial scroll, believed by the Egyptians to give a set of spells and instructions to the deceased for navigating the afterlife. It has nothing to do with Abraham, nor human sacrifice, nor astronomy. In the Egyptian language, it's referred to as the *Sensen* document or permit, which is sometimes translated as *The Book of Breathings*, and is based on a similar book called the *Book of the Dead*, or the *Book of Coming Forth by Day*, which serves a similar purpose.

The Mormon church has published an essay in the last few years admitting that no part of the text of the *Book of Abraham* corresponds to any text in the *Sensen* document that was in Joseph's possession, or any of the other papyri he had available (https://www.lds.org/topics/translation-and-historicity-of-the-book-of-abraham?lang=eng).

> "None of the characters on the papyrus fragments mentioned Abraham's name or any of the events recorded in the book of Abraham. Mormon and non-Mormon Egyptologists agree that the characters on the fragments do not match the translation given in the book of Abraham"

It seems like that alone should be an open-and-shut case. But of course it's not for those who believe Joseph Smith had divine powers of translation. So let's look at other important facts and see where they converge. At the same time, let's look at a number of alternate theories for the translation:

(1) First, a claim has been made by Mormon defenders that perhaps Joseph Smith was simply receiving the text via direct revelation from God and it was never meant to correspond to the Egyptian text. I mean, if that's true, then there's no point in comparing the Egyptian text with Joseph Smith's translation, right?

(2) Additionally, another claim was made that perhaps the translation came from a portion of the papyrus that is no longer extant, or an entirely different scroll altogether. After all, it's certainly possible that the actual text he used has been lost in the last 200 years. There was a fire in a

Chicago museum where at least some of the papyri originally in his possession was destroyed. There's even a record of someone referring to a "long scroll" which we obviously don't have any more. So maybe the text was on that? Pretty convenient explanations, but it's possible, right?

The problem with both of these alternate theories is that they are contradicted by the record of Joseph Smith's scribes working closely with him, the historical documents surrounding the translation, and by Joseph Smith's own journal entries. To the first alternate theory that he believed his translation was just coming from direct revelation and not from the scroll, let's look at Joseph Smith's own record:

> "I commenced the translation of some of the characters or hieroglyphics, and much to our joy found that one of the scrolls contained the writings of Abraham, another the writings of Joseph of Egypt. (History of the Church, 2:236)
>
> "The remainder of this month, I was continually engaged in translating an alphabet of the *Book of Abraham*, and arranging a grammar of the Egyptian language as practiced by the ancients." (History of the Church, 2:238)
>
> "This afternoon I re-commenced translating from the ancient records." (History of the Church, 2:289)

> "In the afternoon we translated some of the Egyptian records." (History of the Church, 2:320) "Spent the day in translating Egyptian characters from the papyrus, though severely afflicted with a cold." (History of the Church, 2:320)

Any alternate theory that supposes Joseph Smith did not believe he was translating ancient Egyptian characters in his possession needs to account for his own record claiming that was *exactly* what he believed he was doing.

For the second theory, it presupposes that he was in fact translating ancient characters, just not the characters from the papyri we still have today. That would be a fair argument if we had no idea what was happening in Joseph Smith's mind at the time. But as it turns out, the Mormon church has published many historical documents that allow us to easily recreate what Joseph Smith thought he was translating. All of the documents I will reference here (collectively known as the Kirtland Egyptian Papers or KEP) are available for review on the Mormon church-owned website josephsmithpapers.org.

(1) First, there is a document known as the Grammar and Alphabet of the Egyptian Language (http://www.josephsmithpapers.org/paper-summary/grammar-and-alphabet-of-the-egyptian-language-circa-july-circa-november-1835/7). This document is also referenced directly by Joseph

Smith in that second journal entry above. Although Mormon defenders frequently try to deflect the importance of the document, it's clear from the title as well as the layout (as well as Joseph Smith's own description of it) what the intention of the document was. Of key interest to us are the first two major entries in the document. The first is a character I'll call the "Chaldean" character: a dot with a vertical line below and two diagonally-up lines extending from the right side of the vertical line. If you read the description next to it, it's clear that the intent was to define this character as something to do with Chaldeans. The description next to it says, "This is called Za Kioan hiash, [or] chal sidon hiash." It's the "chal sidon hiash" that concerns us here. The second character that concerns us is on the second page of text, and looks similar to a semi-colon, a dot with a curved line underneath it. The description next to it says, "Ah brah aam a father of many nations a prince of peace."

(2) Second is a document that shows a copied column of Egyptian text in the handwriting of Joseph's scribe, William Phelps (http://www.josephsmithpapers.org/paper-summary/egyptian-alphabet-circa-early-july-circa-november-1835-c/7). There is another document

with a nearly identical setup, and it was written by Oliver Cowdery, another scribe. On the bottom of both pages are the two characters described in the first document: the "Chaldean" character as well as the "Abraham" character. Written in English right next to the characters are the words "Za ki on hish or Kulsidon hish The land of the Chaldees" followed by "Ah brah oam The father of the faithful". The Convergence of Fact continues to demonstrate Joseph Smith was assigning the meanings of "Chaldees" and "Abraham" to those two characters. And as luck would have it, we still have the original column of Egyptian text that this was copied from. It's the column that immediately follows the first vignette in the *Sensen* document Joseph Smith claimed to be translating from (the vignette Mormons know as Facsimile 1).

(3) Finally, there are three manuscripts of the *Book of Abraham* text, all handwritten by different scribes (http://www.josephsmithpapers.org/paper-summary/book-of-abraham-manuscript-circa-july-circa-november-1835-c-abraham-11-218/1). All three of them stop and start at different points in the text, but all three of them have Egyptian characters lined up with sections of the text. The same exact text lines up with the same exact

Egyptian characters. The C manuscript has the only reference to the beginning of the *Book of Abraham*. And wouldn't you know it, the "Chaldees" and "Abraham" characters are both there next to the opening text reading "In the land of the Chaldeans, at the residence of my fathers, I, Abraham, saw that it was needful for me to obtain another place of residence."

The facts support the claim that not only did Joseph Smith believe he was translating the ancient Egyptian *Sensen* document in his possession, but that we actually know precisely which characters he believed he was translating from. The remainder of the Egyptian characters in the third documents (the *Book of Abraham* manuscripts) correspond *exactly* in sequence with the Egyptian characters immediately following the column of text in the second document. The alternate theories proposed by Mormon defenders simply do not support the claims that he thought he was simply receiving revelation independent of the papyrus, nor do they support the claim that he was translating from some other text now lost to us. And if we're to use parsimony in our list of causal entities, we have a very sufficient explanation for describing what Joseph Smith thought he was doing. We don't need to introduce supernatural inspiration to explain how he did what he did. A supernatural explanation is UNNECESSARY, and it's therefore irrational to conclude.

Of course, Mormon defenders who already know these facts about the historical documents then turn to the text of the *Book of Abraham* itself to argue there are things Joseph Smith simply couldn't have known in the 19th century. (For example, traditional Jewish stories of attempts on Abraham's life when he was young, or that anciently it was believed that Abraham taught astronomy in Egypt.) And their defense for such a position is that these stories don't exist in the Bible. (As though the only book Joseph Smith ever read in his life was the Bible.) Unfortunately for the Mormon defenders, these facts would have been relatively easy for Joseph Smith to learn. The stories about attempts on Abraham's life are available in the Jewish Midrash. And the story about Abraham discussing astronomy in Egypt is found in the writings of Josephus, an ancient Jewish historian. Yes, Joseph Smith had access to both of these. The writings of Josephus are even referenced by Oliver Cowdery (Joseph's scribe) specifically to discuss the papyri acquired by Joseph Smith. In the end, there's simply nothing that NECESSITATES a supernatural explanation for the work Joseph Smith produced, and it is thus irrational to conclude that it has a supernatural source. Every datum of experience surrounding the question can be explained without appeal to a supernatural explanation. And thus, such an explanation is UNNECESSARY and therefore irrational.

Again, those who don't believe the *Book of Abraham* has a supernatural explanation will have already concluded that without the information I have given. Those who believe it has a supernatural explanation won't stop believing based on the information I've given here either. The point is that it is irrational to believe the work has a supernatural basis. In order to make a rational case for the work requiring a supernatural cause, they will need to address the CONVERGENCE OF FACT that points to a very natural, human source for the production, rather than picking and choosing (*Texas sharpshooter*) ONE-HIT WONDER that can themselves be explained via natural means as well. They will also need to demonstrate some MEASUREMENT that NECESSITATES a supernatural explanation. That's how rationality works.

When I started this chapter, I had about 30 different case studies I was ready to address. As I started writing, I realized this chapter would make its own book if I went that route. Some of them related to the "big questions" about the origin of the universe. And on that topic, this is me "bending over backwards" to say that explanations for order within the universe may constitute the closest thing to a rational belief in an intelligent creator that exists. That's not to say that it's rational to conclude an intelligent creator. It only means that the order of the universe needs to be explained. But even if such intelligent creator existed, it would be just as irrational to conclude that it's the Christian god as it would be to conclude it has bat-like wings or wears a monocle and top hat. These are both UNNECESSARY conclusions to make based simply on the order of the universe. And in a number of ways, the irrationality of the Christian god seems to contradict the god hypothesized by the order of the universe anyway. In a similar sense, even if such a being existed, there is no connection between that claim and the claim of Joseph Smith receiving the *Book of Abraham* via divine revelation (\*these are all non sequiturs\*).

Hopefully from these few examples in this chapter, it is relatively clear that the tools of rationality can be used to clearly delineate between rational and irrational claims with relative ease. Each one of these topics would take its own book to cover every conceivable detail. I'm open to discussing each one more fully. But having discussed each of the points I've given here many times with very little response from their usual defenders, I will assume I covered the opposing argument relatively fairly. Belief in the *Book of Abraham* having a supernatural origin is irrational, even if it actually has a supernatural origin. Belief in alien visitations is irrational, even if aliens have actually visited. Belief in the Good Guy with a Gun as a solution to mass killings is approximately 3% rational, and

97% irrational. If the goal is rationality, we need to stop treating the two sides to each argument as having equal weight when one side is not rational. People simply believe some irrational things. We need to get better at removing our emotions from the debate and looking at the specific scenario using the tools of rationality. And then make decisions with the clarity of that rationality.

# Chapter 7 – Conclusion

Hey there! I'm so happy to see you made to the final chapter of the book. Hopefully by this point, we are on the same page, both metaphorically and literally, regarding the incompatible nature of faith-based and rational-based thinking. I've been kind of rough on faith-based thinking, and yet very honest and factual. There are some ways in which the two modes of thinking can happen at the same time, but in so many ways they simply cannot occur in the same brain at the same time.

Because things have been a little rough in this book with respect to faith-based thinking, let me reiterate a positive note I've mentioned several times before. I'm not trying to take your happiness away from you. Many people find peace and solace in their faith-based beliefs. They go to a church or to the top of a mountain to find God, whatever that means for them, and it helps get them through the day as well as through the difficult trials of life. I totally get it. I lived that experience for decades, and I have many friends and family who are right there with you. Inasmuch as faith-based thinking provides a coping mechanism for you, to help wake you up in the morning and get you through the day, don't let me take that from you. I know many wonderful religious people who truly love their fellow humans. Their faith compels them to serve humanity, and they look for opportunities to give because their faith asks it of them. For some people, it provides the inspiration they need to build, create, and do good things in the world. It provides imagination and ideas. Have you seen the inside of the Sistine Chapel or the art inside the ancient Egyptian tombs? Faith-based thinking can be beautiful and inspiring. It gives hope and light despite the darker realities of life.

And again, at no time am I questioning faith in oneself. Such faith may in fact be irrational. Maybe your musical skills aren't cut out for *American Idol*, but so what? Go for it! Live your dream and do what your heart tells you (technically your limbic system, but whatever). You only have one life, so live it. (Disclaimer: some people have the dream to hurt other people. That sort of dream sucks. Don't live that dream. Find a dream that lifts the world and humanity and do that instead.) I don't care what the odds are, my advice to you is to live according to your heart and be happy. Do this. And if you're already doing this, the world needs more people like you. Have faith in yourself, and live your life to the fullest.

Additionally, there are those who are drawn to faith-based thinking, who have a nuanced, thoughtful perspective on their faith. They recognize the absurdity of the supernatural claims, but just really want to believe anyway. In my experience, this group of individuals are highly intelligent, but still quite drawn to matters of the heart. It's not my intention to spoil their beliefs either, especially since they've already run their beliefs through the wringer anyway. These are people who are highly unlikely to use their religious belief to harm others, and I have little to no issue with them. It's okay to have a "thoughtful" faith, as long as it's understood there's no such thing as a "reasonable" faith. If by "thoughtful" you are acknowledging the faith is irrational, then my issue lies elsewhere. I have no problem with those who understand the basis of their faith but wish to believe anyway, so long as faith is not being used to harm others.

Are we squared up on faith in oneself and hope to get you through the day? Are we good? Okay, I need finish by discussing faith-based thinking that isn't necessary to keep your life hanging together by a thread. I need to talk about faith-based thinking that has nothing to do with believing in yourself. I'm talking about the other kind that gets used to make irrational arguments in Congress, such arguments that are used to negatively affect other people's lives. Yes, I'm talking about that now.

For all other types of faith-based thinking, we need to stop sugar coating the relationship between faith and reason.

They are NOT the same thing. They are not the same thing when it comes to areas of brains engaged. They require contradictory processes of thinking. The same person cannot engage in faith-based thinking and rational-based thinking at the same time. It's true that religion is NOT the cause of all the problems in the world. Many problems are simply caused by greedy people who use and harm other people to get what they want. There are a few very rich people with the ability to harm the rest of the world for their own short term gain (I'm not saying all rich people are harmful...back off). But in a democracy, those few greedy people need the votes of at least 51% in order to push their agendas into law. And greedy people with power often get their support of the 51% through faith-based thinking and manipulation of that type of thinking.

If you think you aren't being manipulated by those seeking short term gains at the expense and harm of the long term, take a moment to explain – in your own words – the arguments for and against man-made climate change. Think about whether this is a rational argument for you or an emotional one. (Hint: if you can't even explain what the arguments for and against man-made climate change are, yet you have a very strong opinion about it, you might be getting emotionally manipulated by those who have something to gain by your vote. In any case, if you can't even explain what the arguments are, your strong opinion is de facto irrational.  You are being used.)

Thus, the primary problem with faith-based thinking is that it's touted as a virtue in order to hijack minds.  How can anyone have morals if they don't believe in God, amirite?  Unfortunately, faith-based thinking doesn't give you access to a better moral system.  If anything, it may tie you down to outdated morals.  Faith-based thinking means you use your limbic system to make decisions rather than your prefrontal cortex.  There's nothing about emotional-based thinking that automatically makes it more moral than rational-based thinking.  And there are many reasons why it might be a much more flighty, inconsistent, unfair way of deciding ethical questions.  Within many faith-based religious groups, it's considered a desirable quality to NOT question authority.  It's considered desirable to NOT question absurd ideas.  The anti-intellectual movement in the United States makes it a virtue to cling to an idea precisely because it's not considered intelligent.  And the more absurd an idea is, the more virtuous it is to cling to it (recall the Abraham drinking water discussion from chapter 2).  Remember Voltaire's quote: "Certainly anyone who has the power to make you believe absurdities has the power to make you commit injustices."  As a people, we need to stop allowing the few to hijack minds based on an emotional response to stimuli.

In chapter 2, I argued that there is a 1-to-1 relationship between faith and absurdity. Any scenario where it would be dangerous to rely on absurdity to choose, you should also consider it just as dangerous to use faith to choose. However, let me "bend over backwards" to state that not all absurdity is bad. The point of this book is not to say remove all absurdity from your life. There is a purpose for absurdity. We need an All Fool's Day and a Saturnalia to flip the usual social conventions on their heads every now and again. When my daughter was very young, I used to make absurd jokes to help teach critical thinking skills. After she knew her numbers, I would start counting, "One, three, four, five," in order for her to use her critical thinking skills to catch the mistake. I think Lewis Carroll's *Alice's Adventures in Wonderland* serves a similar purpose. But the value from this absurdity comes from recognizing the absurdity, not living inside of it as though the absurdity is rational. Absurdity is like a drug, and through it we can find a catharsis by diving into the world of the irrational every now and again. But there's a time and place for it. Public policy is NOT that place.

Lastly, let me reiterate once again that I recognize there are those who need faith to keep them going. However, in chapter 2 I had recommended weaning yourself off the "faith sauce", even if you need it right now to keep yourself alive and motivated. Find ways to ease out of the need to believe in absurd things to keep you motivated. Dumbo never needed the feather to fly. You do not need faith-based thinking to keep you going or to keep you happy, even if it'll take a little bit to bring you to that point. At first, it's a little terrifying to let go of the "faith sauce" just as it's terrifying to let go of the bottle if you have a drinking problem. The withdrawal symptoms can be rough for both. I asked you not to sugar coat the relationship between faith and reason, and so I'll do the same here. Leaving faith-based thinking is not easy. But I can assure you it's better and brighter and clearer on the other side of the pain of letting go of it than it is from within faith-based thinking.

At the very least, it's certainly more logical. All the time, I hear religious people fretting and worrying about how God's will doesn't make sense. They've tried to live according to their religion's rules, and it often seems like God blesses the heathen more than he helps them. Such faith-based thinking can be incredibly frustrating. But it's also incredibly frustrating, and the consequences of their faith-based actions will likely never make sense, because events in their lives are probably just random occurrence. It's a very strong possibility that all the events that happen to you are just White Noise interpreted as divine will. But when you remove the UNNECESSARY assumption that God is testing you from within the White Noise, the world is infinitely more clear and comprehensible. When that mental shift happens, suddenly all of the confusion of strange happenstance and coincidence dissipates. And then it hits you: knowing HOW TO THINK really does feel good.

Made in the USA
Las Vegas, NV
19 June 2021